The Angels and Us

4/19-jw ?x

ALSO BY MORTIMER J. ADLER

The Angels and Us

by

Mortimer J. Adler

COLLIER BOOKS
Macmillan Publishing Company / *New York*

Maxwell Macmillan Canada / *Toronto*

Maxwell Macmillan International
New York   Oxford   Singapore   Sydney

Collier Books
Macmillan Publishing Company
866 Third Avenue
New York, NY 10022

Maxwell Macmillan Canada, Inc.
1200 Eglinton Avenue East
Suite 200
Don Mills, Ontario M3C 3N1

Macmillan Publishing Company is part of the Maxwell Communication Group of Companies.

Library of Congress Cataloging-in-Publication Data
Adler, Mortimer Jerome, 1902–
    The angels and us/by Mortimer J. Adler.
        p. cm.
    Originally published: New York: Macmillan, c1982.
    Includes index.
    ISBN 0-02-030065-4
    1. Angels. 2. Angels—History of doctrines. I. Title.
[BT962.A35 1993]   93–1377   CIP
235'.3—dc20

Macmillan books are available at special discounts for bulk purchases for sales promotions, premiums, fund-raising, or educational use. For details, contact:

Special Sales Director
Macmillan Publishing Company
866 Third Avenue
New York, NY 10022

First Collier Books Edition 1988

10 9 8 7 6 5 4 3 2 1

Printed in the United States of America

Contents

[vii]

Preface

WHEN, in 1943, Robert Hutchins and I undertook to edit *Great Books of the Western World* for the Encyclopaedia Britannica company, I also worked on constructing a systematic guide to the discussion of the great ideas by the authors of the great books. The first task in the construction of the *Syntopicon*, which became the title of that guide, involved the selection of the ideas to be treated and the formulation of the topics to be considered under each idea.

By 1945, after working for two years with collaborators, I settled upon a final list of 102 ideas. My recollection is that I had little difficulty in getting my associates' approval of almost all the ideas I proposed to include. But I also remember that I stood almost alone in my insistence on the inclusion of the idea of ANGEL.

The task fell to me of writing an essay about each of the great ideas that were to become chapters in the *Syntopicon*. Deciding to adopt an alphabetical order for the presentation of the ideas, I wrote the essay on ANGEL first, and sent copies of my first draft to Mr. Hutchins, who was then President of the University of Chicago, and to Senator William Benton, who was then publisher of *Enyclopaedia Britannica*.

I will never forget Senator Benton's immediate reaction. He was flabbergasted by my choice of ANGEL as one of the great ideas. He thought it did not belong in that company at all. What made matters worse was the prominence given it by putting it first.

Mr. Hutchins, some members of the Editorial Advisory Board, and my immediate associates in the work of producing the *Syntopicon* were also querulous about the inclusion of ANGEL, but not in such a temper about it as Senator Benton.

I persisted. My reading of the great books had persuaded me that ANGEL should be included among the great ideas. The *Syntopicon* was published in 1952 with ANGEL its opening chapter. The essay I wrote on that subject ran to about 5,000 words and barely skirted the surface of the subject that is treated at much greater length in the present volume.

Writing this book has further persuaded me that I was right in my judgment thirty-five years ago. Reading it, I hope, will persuade others that that is the case.

In the years subsequent to the completion of the *Syntopicon* and the publication of *Great Books of the Western World*, I have lectured on angels before a variety of audiences—the students in St. John's College at Annapolis and in the downtown college of the University of Chicago; the designers working for Steuben Glass, who considered making crystal angels in the round but found it easier to make them in bas-relief; and, on other occasions, popular audiences across the country.

On all these occasions, I found that the subject had the same fascination for others that it did for me, a fascination that was in no way affected by the heterodox beliefs of the persons listening or diminished by the absence or denial of any religious belief.

The most recent occasion occurred several summers ago in Aspen, Colorado, where I give an annual lecture under the auspices of the Aspen Institute for Humanistic Studies. The announcement of a lecture on angels and angelology drew an audience larger than any I have ever enjoyed in the last thirty years. The auditorium was filled to overflowing and the spirited discussion following the lecture ran for almost an hour. The range and character of the questions asked and the penetration of some

of the points raised testified amply to the fascination of the subject for everyone involved.

   It was then that I decided to write this book.

Aspen, Colorado   M.J.A.
June 1981

The Angels and Us

PART ONE

Prologue

1

The Fascination of
Angels

(1) *Minds Without Bodies*

BODIES without minds—nothing unusual about that. Except
for the adherents of a strange doctrine known as panpsychism,*
it would not occur to anyone to think things might be otherwise.
The spectacle of bodies without minds does not have the fascination of the odd or abnormal.

Equally familiar and calling as little for special notice are minds
associated with bodies in various forms of animal life, including
the human. But minds without bodies—that is, indeed, an extraordinary prospect. Therein lies the fascination of angels.

Nothing has greater fascination for the human mind than

---

*The theory that every physical thing has some degree of consciousness or
mentality.

manifestations, supposed or real, of something akin to human intelligence in non-human beings. This accounts for our interest in the minds of other animals and even for our tendency to exaggerate the mental powers we attribute to them, especially to domesticated animals and household pets.

Our fascination with intelligence apart from our own is intensified when the minds conjectured or imagined are thought to be superior, and especially if they do not have the limitations imposed upon the human mind by its association with the frailties of the human body.

Angels as objects of religious belief and of theological or philosophical speculation represent only one form of such fascination with superhuman intelligence. For many centuries of Western civilization and until recently, it was the only form. It was preceded in antiquity by mythological figures to whom superhuman powers were attributed and by the all-too-human gods and demigods of the polytheistic religions of the ancient world. These anthropomorphic deities were, perhaps, the oldest expression of man's interest in the superhuman.

Angelology, which is the subject of this book, is speculation about minds, either totally without bodies or with bodies that they take on as guises but do not inhabit. Call angelology "theology-fiction" or "philosophy-fiction" if you like, or regard it as a legitimate part of theology as queen of the sciences and of philosophy as her handmaiden. However you look upon it, be prepared to acknowledge at least that it can exercise a fascination for us comparable to that of contemporary speculations or fantasies about other forms of superhuman intelligence.

I claim for it more than that. I will try to show that angels are the most fascinating of all such objects of fantasy and thought because, unlike all other forms of superhuman intelligence that fall short of the infinite power of a divine intellect, angels—and angels alone—are minds without bodies.

Anything that belongs to the cosmos, when that is understood as the totality of everything physical, must have corporeality or be associated with corporeality. No matter how fantastic are the bodily forms and powers of the aliens of outer space invented by science fiction, the intelligence of these imaginary figures operates through and with physical appendages.

Since the forms of extraterrestrial life and intelligence that some twentieth-century cosmologists think may inhabit the far reaches of our galaxy and beyond still fall within the cosmos as a whole, such minds will certainly have bodies. They will probably be endowed with nervous systems and brains that, however superior in degree to our own, cannot be totally unlike the physical organs upon which the operation of the human mind seems to depend.

Again, angels—minds without bodies—are the striking exception. They are not merely forms of extraterrestrial intelligence. They are forms of extra-cosmic intelligence.

(2) *Extraterrestrial Intelligences*

From the fifth century B.C. right down to the present day, philosophers and scientists have engaged in speculation about the existence and role of souls or minds in association with or as inhabitants of heavenly bodies—the stars and other planets than earth.

The context of these speculations is cosmological, not theological. They stem either from an effort to explain the motions of the celestial spheres or in response to questions about the structure of the physical cosmos as a whole. Earlier speculations differ in two respects from similar conjectures by twentieth-century cosmologists.

For one thing, earlier speculations occurred before astronomical inquiry had the telescopic instruments to expand its exploration of the cosmos beyond the solar system and the starry heavens visible to the naked eye. For another, the extraterrestrial intelligences were conceived as incorporeal—as spiritual substances—even though they were also thought to be attached to heavenly bodies either as their motive forces or as their animating principles.

We need not go into the details of Aristotle's pre-Copernican astronomy to understand the role that these extraterrestrial intelligences played. They were postulated by him as celestial motors to explain the regular and everlasting motion of the celestial spheres in perfectly circular orbits.

Everlasting motion, in Aristotle's view, could not be explained except by the everlasting action of a cause that performed this action without being acted on—an unmoved mover, in short. But, in addition to a prime mover, itself unmoved, Aristotle also thought that each of the celestial spheres required its own unmoved mover to account for its endless revolution. These secondary unmoved movers Aristotle conceived as intelligences that functioned as motors for the spheres to which they are attached.

In order to be causes of motion without themselves being moved, they had to be incorporeal agents. For Aristotle, an incorporeal agent could be nothing other than a mind or intelligence.

While he sometimes used the word "God" as a synonym for the prime mover of the physical cosmos, his meaning for that term differed in one crucial respect from the understanding of the deity in the Judaeo-Christian and Islamic religions of the West. Aristotle's prime mover did not create the cosmos that its agency maintained in everlasting motion. It preserved the motion of the spheres, but it did not preserve the existence of the cosmos.

His conception of the function performed by the celestial intelligences that were secondary unmoved movers differed as radically from the Judaeo-Christian and Islamic view of the role played by angels in the divine scheme of things. It is a serious mistake to suppose, as is supposed by some modern critics of angelology, that the theory of angels in the three great religions of the West was adopted from or even influenced by the now completely discarded, outmoded cosmology of antiquity.

In the late sixteenth and early seventeenth centuries, the great post-Copernican astronomer Johannes Kepler dealt a death blow to the Aristotelian world picture. This completed the revolution begun by the Copernican attack upon Ptolemy. Even more consequential than the replacement of the geocentric by the heliocentric hypothesis, with the planets orbiting around the sun instead of the celestial spheres circling around the earth, was Kepler's rejection of the Aristotelian and Ptolemaic supposition that the matter composing the heavenly bodies differed radically from terrestrial matter. With it went the erroneous notion that the heavenly bodies were incorruptible, subject only to change of place and to no other mode of change, along with the equally erroneous notion that their movements were always perfectly circular.

Kepler's precise mathematical description of the elliptical pathways of the planets in their orbiting around the sun rested on massive observational data accumulated by Tycho Brahe. In the closing pages of his treatise on *Harmonies of the World*, Kepler disclaims any need to introduce either "god-intelligences" as Aristotle did, or "armies of innumerable planetary spirits" as the Magi did. Nevertheless, he reports Tycho Brahe's opinion that the globes other than this earth "are filled with inhabitants"; and he concludes by asking whether God had so exhausted his creative powers in peopling this planet with various forms of life "that he was unable . . . to adorn the other globes too with their fitting creatures?"

William Gilbert, another early scientist, living and writing at the same time, regarded the magnetic force (which was the subject of his investigation) as animate, imitating the human soul and even surpassing it. In the concluding pages of his treatise *On the Loadstone and Magnetic Bodies*, Gilbert discusses what he takes to be Aristotle's hypothesis—that the heavenly bodies are animated by souls—not to reject it, but rather to correct it by attributing a soul as well to the planet earth, which so plainly manifests the action of magnetism.

Still another type of speculation concerning souls or minds

inhabiting other portions of the cosmos occurred a century later. The following passage appears in the works of Lord Bolingbroke:

> We cannot doubt that numberless worlds and systems of worlds compose this amazing whole, the universe; and as little, I think, that the planets which roll about the sun, or those which roll about a multitude of others, are inhabited by living creatures, fit to be inhabitants of them. When we have this view before our eyes, can we be stupid or vain or impertinent enough to imagine that we stand alone or foremost among rational created beings?

Influenced either directly by Bolingbroke, or by the reflection of Bolingbroke's thought in Alexander Pope's *Essay on Man*, which he read and admired, the great German philosopher Immanuel Kant lectured mankind about the modest position occupied by the human species in the cosmic scheme. "Human nature," Kant declared,

> occupies, as it were, the middle rung of the Scale of Being, . . . equally removed from the two extremes. If the contemplation of the most sublime classes of rational creatures, which inhabit Jupiter or Saturn, arouses [man's] envy and humiliates him with a sense of his own inferiority, he may again find contentment and satisfaction by turning his gaze upon those lower grades which, in the planets Venus and Mercury, are far below the perfection of human nature.

Similar conjecturing comes to us from still another source a century later. Karl Barth's extensive discussion of the Kingdom of Heaven (in his *Church Dogmatics*, Volume III) calls attention to a number of relatively obscure German theologians in the nineteenth century who gave reasons for thinking it highly probable that elsewhere in the universe there are intelligent creatures superior to man.

One of these, Volkmar Reinhard, writing in 1812, argued that "since the heavenly bodies, whose number and size are almost immeasurable, . . . cannot possibly be left untenanted by God, but are incontestably filled with creatures appropriate to their nature, we are freely justified in assuming a host and variety of creatures infinitely surpassing all human conception."

This theme is repeated, with a number of variations played upon it, by K. G. Bretschneider in 1838 and by Richard Rothe in 1870, down to Adolf Schlatter in 1923 and Ernst Troeltsch in 1925. Throughout this series of theological treatises, some attempt is made to relate the hypothesis of superior intelligences inhabiting other parts of the physical universe with the Biblical doctrine of God's heavenly host of holy angels.

It is easy to see why some connection between the two might be supposed. The one thread that connects them is the attribution to these hypothetical beings of intellects superior to that possessed by man. On the other hand, it is not always clear that these superior intellects are minds without bodies. That certainly does not enter into the conjectures of Carl Sagan and others who, in the twentieth century, have defended the probability of extraterrestrial life and intelligence.

Furthermore, in all the theorizing that has so far been recounted, the intellects whose existence is postulated, with or without bodies, either have a special location in one or another celestial body or have a special attachment to different portions of the physical cosmos.

In these two very important respects, they are not the angels of Biblical lore and of Western religious belief; nor are they immaterial substances that, as unembodied intellects, become the objects of philosophical thought.

Nevertheless, it is necessary to note an affinity between the arguments advanced by Lord Bolingbroke and others in the eighteenth century (for the existence in the universe of intellects superior to the human mind) and the arguments for the existence of angels (to which we will come in Chapter 4). What is common to both is the assumption that the hierarchy or scale of beings in the universe would be rendered defective if man, at the summit of the ascending scale of earthly creatures, did not have above him another series of gradations in being that ascended upward from man's middle position in the cosmic scheme, thus filling the gap between man and God.

When this affinity is noted, it also remains necessary to note that all the speculation about extraterrestrial intelligences, from Aristotle to Sagan, falls within the context of thinking about the structure and functions of the physical cosmos. For Sagan and his contemporaries, it is not the argument from gradations of being but rather the probability of biophysical and biochemical conditions favorable to extraterrestrial life that underlies guesses about the presence of intelligent life elsewhere in the cosmos.

In sharp contrast, the Biblical testimony about angels, together with theological speculations about their nature and operation, falls within the context of thinking about God and about what Divine providence has ordained for the glory of God and the salvation of man.

(3) *The Image of Angels*

It is only by overlooking obvious discrepancies that philosophical and scientific speculation about extraterrestrial beings endowed with intelligence, embodied or not, can be considered as having a significant bearing on the existence, nature, and mission of angels.

The philosophers and scientists who have engaged in such speculations clearly do not have angels in mind—certainly not the angels that make their appearance in the Old Testament, the New Testament, and the Koran.

Exactly the opposite statement must be made about the painters and poets who have delineated them or made reference to them. The images they have provided us plainly reflect what they have imbibed from the legends and lore, as well as the doctrines and dogmas, of the three great Western religions.

Influenced by Western painting and poetry from the thirteenth century to the present day, our imagination responds by picturing winged figures robbed in dazzling white and having some resemblance to the bodily aspect, especially the facial vis-

age, of human beings. This image, shared by believers and unbelievers, contains features that represent some of the elements
of meaning in the abstract conception of angels to be found in
the writings of Jewish, Christian, and Islamic theologians.

The human appearance suggests that angels, like men, are
persons—that they are most essentially characterized by their intelligence. The wings, sometimes only a pair and sometimes more
numerous, suggest the function of angels—their service as messengers from God to man. That, by the way, is the literal meaning of the Hebrew and the Greek words that become "angel" in
English. Not all angels, as we shall see, serve as messengers, but
the most frequent reference to them in Sacred Scriptures de-
scribes them as performing this mission.

The aura of light that surrounds them, especially the haloes
that encircle their heads, suggest a quite different role. Their
wings betoken their coming to mankind as messengers, but their
haloes symbolize that they come from Heaven which is their
home.

They belong to the unearthly kingdom of God, not to the
earthly domain inhabited by man and other corporeal creatures.
They may come to earth to perform their missions, but they
never remain there for long. As members of the heavenly host,
the primary direction of their gaze is toward God, not toward
man.

The imagery of dazzling, often blinding, light also symbolizes
the spirituality of angels. Pure spirits, totally incorporeal beings,
cannot be painted, nor can they be described in words that call
images to mind. Only by using the symbolism of light, which
makes the invisible visible, can painters and poets try to prevent
an egregious misunderstanding of the imagery they are compelled to employ. The bodily forms and features that they depict
angels as having must be recognized as pictorial metaphors, not
as literal representations of what angels are like.

I cannot postpone mentioning a matter to which I will return
in a later chapter when I attempt to expound angelology as a
branch of sacred theology. Theologians must take account of the

bodily appearance of angels in Sacred Scriptures, sometimes in human form and dress, so that they are initially mistaken to be men; and sometimes garbed in white, with wings, haloes, and flashing swords. Holding firm to the thesis that angels are purely spiritual beings, theologians explain their corporeal forms and aspects as merely instrumental to the performance of their mission as messengers from God.

The explanation involves a fundamental negation, without which the immateriality of angels would be contradicted. The bodies they appear to have are not really bodies or indispensable to their life, as the bodies you and I have are really bodies and indispensable to us. Not only are we unable to live our earthly lives without bodies, but the bodies we have are truly organic, performing a variety of vital functions, including vegetative ones.

Not so the bodies that angels appear to have. In the language of the theologians, their corporeal forms are merely "assumed bodies," bodies that are not truly organic. They perform no vital functions, certainly not the vegetative ones.

In addition, these assumed bodies are taken on by angels as guises only for the sake of engaging in their earthly ministry. Useful for that purpose, they are totally dispensable and, furthermore, must be dispensed with. When angels return to their heavenly home, the resumption of their normal life as members of the heavenly host not only can, but must, discard every vestige of corporeality.

The great Reformed theologian, Karl Barth, in the extraordinary treatment of angelology set forth in that portion of his *Church Dogmatics* devoted to the Kingdom of Heaven, has good reason to complain of the trifling, merely ornamental, and often childish notions about angels that Christian painting and poetry are responsible for obtruding into our consciousness. "Here as elsewhere," he writes, Christian art "is responsible for so much that is inappropriate."

While conceding that "there are tolerable and in their way moving and instructive representations of the specifically child-like angel," Barth deplores paintings that depict "the infant Jesus with a veritable kindergarten of prancing babies amusing themselves in different ways and yet all contriving in some way to look pious. Even more offensive are Raphael's little darlings." He goes on to say that "it would be a good thing if diminutives like the German *Engelein* and the English 'cherub,' with all the false associations that they evoke, could be banished from current usage. The same holds true of the common conception of angels as charming creatures."

Barth's wishing to banish certain misleading references to angels in speech and certain demeaning depictions of angels in painting reminds us of Plato's wish to expel poets and painters from the ideal state because their portrayal of the gods so grievously misrepresents them.

It also reminds us of the second commandment that enjoins us not to make graven images. Images, whether carved in stone, painted on a canvas, or formed by words, must necessarily be inappropriate—or worse, distortions—when we undertake to contemplate totally incorporeal, purely spiritual, objects, such as God and his holy angels. Strictly speaking, they are objects of thought, not of imagination.

Be that as it may, the use of our imagination still remains unavoidable, if only because the delineation of angels in Sacred Scriptures cannot be read without summoning up the images the words evoke. It inevitably leads to pictorial representations of them when religious themes become the preoccupation of great painters and poets, as they most certainly have in Western civilization.

Nor can it be gainsaid that a large part of our fascination with angels derives from immersion in the imagery of angels that we encounter in the galleries of any great museum and from our recollection of angels as heroic figures in such great epic poems as Dante's *Divine Comedy*, Milton's *Paradise Lost*, and Goethe's *Faust*, not to mention the memorable lines devoted to angels in countless lyrics.

The great scenes and moments in the Biblical narrative that have been recurrent subjects of Western painting include angels either as central figures in the episode or as an essential part of the background.

They occur in pictures of Abraham's being deterred by an angel from sacrificing his son Isaac, notably by Andrea del Sarto, Rembrandt, and Titian; in portrayals by Raphael, Rembrandt, and Murillo of the visit of three angels to Abraham; in Raphael's painting of Jacob's dream of the ladder stretching from earth to heaven on which angels are ascending and descending; and in pictures by Rembrandt and Rubens of the angel who commanded Hagar in the desert to turn back and return to Abraham.

The New Testament provides Christian artists with an even larger number of themes involving the action or presence of angels: paintings by Raphael, Veronese, Perugino, Tintoretto, and Rubens of the baptism of Christ; Perugino's portrayal of the temptation of Christ by Satan, in which holy angels hover at Christ's feet; representations of the ascension and resurrection of Christ by Giotto and Correggio; and pictures of the angel rolling the stone away from Christ's tomb.

Nearly every great artist of the Renaissance or at least leading representatives of every major school painted the Annunciation in which the angel of the Lord brings the glad tidings to the Virgin Mary; this is almost equally true of such themes as the nativity of Christ, the adoration of the Magi, and the infant Jesus reclining on the lap of Mary.

In addition, there are paintings by Murillo of a single guardian angel; by Fra Angelico of an angelic host; by Raphael of the Archangel Michael casting Satan out of heaven; by Botticelli of the Archangel Raphael, and also by him a picture of the Madonna surrounded by angels.

In addition to playing central or significant roles in the great epic poems of Dante, Milton, and Goethe, angels are celebrated in a variety of ways by the writers of English lyrics, from Shakespeare, John Donne, and Henry Vaughan to Dante Gabriel Rossetti, Henry W. Longfellow, Leight Hunt, Emily Dickinson, Edna St. Vincent Millay, and Robert Bridges.

Mentioning Leigh Hunt and remembering how Abou Ben Adhem awoke one night to see "an angel writing in a book of gold," only later to discover that his own name led the list inscribed therein, I cannot refrain from quoting a verse by B. J. Boothroyd that comments on Hunt's poem:

> Abou Ben Adhem's name led all the rest . . .
> Prompting a thesis wildly theoretical
> That even recording angels find it best
> To keep us alphabetical.

Nor can I refrain from calling attention to a witty verse by Lord Byron:

> The angels all were singing out of tune,
> And hoarse with having little else to do,
> Excepting to wind up the sun and moon,
> Or curb a runaway young star or two.

We can never forget that, in the closing lines of Hamlet, Shakespeare has Horatio pay farewell to Hamlet thus: "Good night, sweet prince: and flights of angels sing thee to thy rest." Equally memorable is Milton's "Look homeward, Angel, now, and melt with ruth."

The name of Blake cannot be omitted from this recital. In illustrating Dante's *Divine Comedy*, Milton's *Paradise Lost*, Bunyan's *Pilgrim's Progress*, as well as the Book of Job, Blake was, after Albrecht Dürer, probably the greatest graphic artist depicting angels in the widest variety of shapes, miens, and postures. His famous long poem, "The Marriage of Heaven and Hell," signalled his rejection of views of Heaven and Hell that he had earlier adopted from Emanuel Swedenborg, the Swedish mystical theologian. With them, he abandoned his admiration for angels. "I have always found," he wrote, "that angels have the vanity to speak of themselves as the only wise; this they do with a confident insolence sprouting from systematic reasoning."

Nearer our own time, the theosophical visions of Rudolf Steiner and the poems of Rainer Maria Rilke are as replete with angels as are the visionary writings and the poems of William Blake. A recent commentary on the personality and work of the Oxford philosopher and essayist Isaiah Berlin recounts an interview with him in which the writer, himself deeply absorbed in Rilke's poetry, discussed angels with Berlin. "I came away," he wrote, "convinced that he knew more about angels than I ever should."

There seems to be no end to the fascination of angels or to the unexpected corners and corridors of art and letters in which we may encounter them.

2

The Significance of Angels

(1) *Significance for Whom?*

FOR everyone or only for some? Significant in what context? And under what circumstances?

Let me begin by answering the last of these questions as follows: significant under the circumstances of contemporary life, in the light of our present scientific knowledge of the world and in relation to the present state of both philosophical thought and religious belief.

That the subject of angels was rich in import and freighted with meaning for an earlier epoch is a matter of historic record. Throughout the Middle Ages and into the first centuries of the modern era, the importance of the subject would not have been questioned. Differences of opinion abounded, which made angelology a field of controversy among theologians in the Jewish, Islamic, and Christian religious communities. The very existence of these controversies left little room for doubt about the seriousness and importance of the subject.

Today, of course, the very opposite state of affairs prevails. Doubts abound on all sides and angelology is no longer a major sphere of inquiry or dispute among contemporary theologians of any religious persuasion. It would appear to be a dead subject, of interest only to historians, and of limited interest even to them.

The reader will realize at once that if I agreed with that judgment I would not be engaged in writing this book. While I would not claim that the consideration of angels will ever be attended

by the intellectual excitement that it aroused in the Middle Ages,
I hope I can show that it is still a lively, not a dead, subject, and
one of sufficient significance for everyone to deserve everyone's
attention.

When I say "everyone," I am obviously including the pagans
among us—the disbelievers or unbelievers—as well as those who
are persons of religious faith, communicants in one or another
of the three great Western religions.

For the latter, of course, the significance of angels is predominantly or exclusively in the context or sphere of theological inquiry. The perusal of Sacred Scriptures, wherein angels are so
frequently mentioned, raises questions for anyone who reads the
Old or New Testament or the Koran with the religious faith that
it is the revealed word of God but who also realizes that such
reading must be accompanied by understanding—by some elu-
cidation of the meaning of the text. The process of interpretation, whether carried on spasmodically by the layman or
systematically by the expert, is theological inquiry. It is faith
seeking understanding.

The significance of angels in the context of theology does not
touch the minds of unbelievers or disbelievers, non-religious
persons of whatever variety. For them theology is a closed book,
to be dismissed out of hand or ridiculed as a mass of supersti-
tions. But theology is not the only context in which the significance of angels is to be explored. If it were, the subject would
have a limited audience in the twentieth century.

The other and, in my judgment, equally important context is
that of philosophical thought. If I persist in the opinion that
angels should be of interest to everyone, not only to some, I do
so in the firm conviction, which I have so frequently expressed,
that philosophy is everybody's business.

It might even be said that the philosophical context has a wider
appeal. The questions about angels there to be considered have
interest for persons of religious faith as well as for those lacking
it. Religious faith does not absolve anyone from the obligation

to philosophize—the obligation of anyone with a mind to inquire about matters that lie beyond the reach of scientific investigation.

(2) *Reality or Possibility*

The significance of any subject we may be engaged in considering lies in the questions it elicits that we feel called upon to answer.

When angels are mentioned, the question that usually pops into people's minds today is how many of them can stand on the head of a pin. That question was never propounded by any mediaeval theologian. It was an invention of modern scoffers who used it to exemplify what they regarded as the utterly specious disputes involved in angelology.

Though that mock question never was asked, it does have, indirectly, a serious answer, one that follows from the consideration of how an angel, lacking a body, occupies a particular place. So far as I know, the one right answer occasioned no dispute among mediaeval theologians.

When angels are mentioned, the first question that should pop into everyone's minds is whether or not they really exist. That, by the way, is the first question to be asked about any subject proposed for consideration, or any object of thought. Is it merely an object of thought, or does it also exist in reality, outside our minds and independent of our thinking about it?

Persons of religious faith may not be prone to ask this question. They may contend that there is no need for them to answer it, on the ground that the reality of angels has been vouchsafed for them by Divine revelation. The articles of their religious faith, derived from the text of the Holy Scripture, includes the existence of angels as well as the existence of God.

Nevertheless, theologians attempt to advance arguments for the existence of God. So, too, as we shall see, they attempt to advance arguments for the existence of angels. However, the question remains whether these arguments are strictly theologi-

cal or philosophical. If they are strictly theological, in the sense
that they presuppose the substance of religious faith, then they
will hardly be persuasive to the pagans among us.

For unbelievers, even those with open minds, no strictly theological argument can have any weight. It rests upon a faith they
do not possess. Disbelievers, those of atheistic or agnostic persuasion, reject the notion that there can be cogent philosophical
arguments for the existence of God, even less so for existence of
angels.

Since for them the reality of angels cannot be affirmed, either
by faith or by reason, what use or point can there be in thinking
about angels? If, in exploring the significance of any subject
whatsoever, the first question to be asked is whether it exists in
reality, arriving at a negative answer would seem to preclude the
asking of any further questions. Why, then, bother a moment
further about angels? Nonexistent, they are totally without
significance.

To accept this as a conclusion would conclude this book in a
hurry. It would certainly narrow its scope, limiting it to persons
of religious faith and restricting the significance of angels to the
theological context.

However, the philosophical context remains even if angels do
not really exist but nevertheless remain genuine possibilities. It
must, of course, be shown by philosophical argument that there
is nothing at all impossible about incorporeal or immaterial substances—about minds without bodies. Once that is done, a whole
host of questions arise concerning the properties or attributes of
such possible beings, as well as questions about the manner in
which they operate and the functions they can perform.

Granted that it is quite proper for philosophy, as it may not
be for science or theology, to explore the realm of the merely
possible, the reader who rejects the reality of angels may still be
inclined to ask, Why bother? What of it? Why should we be
concerned with the mere possibility of angels? It certainly cannot be of any practical importance. All the practical problems

we confront occur in the real world, the world in which we have to act, not the realm of the possible.

Practical importance it may not have, but that does not preclude its having significance of another sort—significance for the understanding of ourselves. That is why, as its title indicates, this book is not just about angels. It is a book about angels *and* us.

If man is neither an angel nor a brute, but occupies a middle ground between the real world of material things and the world, either real or possible, of purely spiritual beings, then a right understanding of human nature requires us to avoid lowering man's stature to the level of brutes, while not trying to raise it to the level of angels.

For that purpose, an exploration of the nature and actions of angels is necessary in order to avoid serious errors that have occurred in Western thought as a result of attributing to man traits and powers that are angelic rather than human. At the same time, recognizing what affinities there are between angels and human beings will help us to avoid the equally serious errors that have occurred in Western thought as a result of thinking that man's traits and powers do not differ from those of subhuman animals except in degree.

The philosophical significance of angels is unaffected by denials of their real existence. The exploration of the possibility of angels suffices for the purpose of correcting those errors about human nature that have arisen from failure to understand that man is neither angel nor brute.

Nor is the philosophical significance of angels affected by the affirmation of their reality, affirmation as an article of faith, with or without the support of strictly theological arguments. The character of the possibility remains the same whether angels are regarded merely as objects of thought or are asserted to have actual existence in reality as well.

However, certain questions have been asked about the nature, properties, and actions of angels that do not arise from a consideration of them as merely possible beings. Questions of this sort spring from what is said about angels in Sacred Scripture and from the effort of theologians to interpret the texts in which they are mentioned. We must, therefore, try to draw a line that separates the strictly theological questions appropriate to the reality of angels that is affirmed by religious faith from the purely philosophical questions appropriate to angels as merely possible objects of thought.

That should also help us to eliminate from further consideration much that belongs to the accumulated lore about angels that is neither strictly theological nor purely philosophical. The literature of this subject is filled with the wildest speculations and fantasies of all sorts that go far beyond the reach of either faith or reason.

In addition, the great theological treatises of the Middle Ages, in which angelology is so important and extensive a part, include much that is purely philosophical along with what is strictly theological. They do so as if it were all of one piece. Failure to separate the questions that belong exclusively to theology from those that belong to philosophy cannot help but confuse those who approach the subject from the angle of religious faith as well as those who, lacking such faith, have interest only in matters that reason can explore.

(3) *Theology or Philosophy*

On the one hand, theology is concerned with angels as objects of religious belief, declared by dogma and affirmed by faith as having real existence in the universe created by God.

On the other hand, philosophy is concerned with angels as objects of speculative thought, looked upon as capable of real existence even if they do not actually exist. As objects of thought, they represent a possible type of being to be considered and to be compared with known actualities, principally human beings.

While this indicates some of the points involved in drawing a line between the spheres of theology and philosophy, it does not

by itself suffice to separate the questions about angels that are
exclusively theological and those that arise in the mind of the
philosopher who has no way of knowing whether angels really
exist but who entertains the possibility of their existence.

The *Summa Theologica* of St. Thomas Aquinas, written in the
thirteenth century at the height of the Middle Ages, presented a
clear resolution of the much disputed question about the difference and relation between theology and philosophy. In its opening pages, devoted to the nature of Sacred Doctrine (which was
Aquinas' name for sacred or dogmatic theology), St. Thomas
defined the scope of theological inquiry in terms of the principles upon which it rested—the dogmas of the Church, which are
the articles of Christian faith that have their ultimate warrant in
the acceptance of Sacred Scripture as the revealed word of God.

The principles of sacred or dogmatic theology are revealed
truths, not truths derived from experience or formulated by reason. In sharp contrast, the principles of philosophy are all truths
of the latter sort—none in any way dependent on Divine revelation. Regarding the truths of revelation as superior to those of
reason and experience, because they come from a higher source,
Aquinas espoused the view prevalent in his day, that sacred
theology is the queen of the sciences, and philosophy her
handmaiden.

This must not be misunderstood as relegating philosophy entirely to the role of servant in the household of theology. Having
an independent foundation in the truths naturally known by reason's reflection on the common experience of mankind, philosophy has a life of its own quite apart from the service it may
perform in relation to theology.

It had such a life in antiquity prior to and apart from any
acknowledgment of Divine revelation in the Old and New Testament and in the Koran. It continued to enjoy that independent
status in a later culture when dogmatic theology came into existence for the sake of the understanding that faith seeks to achieve
concerning the dogmas that it accepts. In that process, philosophical thought serves—in fact, is indispensable to—theology,

at least to a theology that is essentially speculative rather than mystical.

Without engaging in philosophical reflection, analysis, and reasoning, the theologian cannot achieve the understanding of religious dogmas or articles of faith that is the goal of his effort. He must, of course, be careful not to try to prove by reason truths that have their sole warrant in revelation. There were, in the Middle Ages, rationalists who tried to do precisely that, notably Peter Abelard, who suffered condemnation for this mistake.

There were also fideists who went to the opposite extreme, abandoning the speculative enterprise entirely and foregoing the benefits—the understanding—that can be achieved for faith only through a disciplined use of reason.

When faith and reason are properly associated, each having a certain measure of autonomy and acknowledging certain limitations, they produce a sacred theology that is both dogmatic in its principles and speculative in its development. In the *Summa Theologica* of Thomas Aquinas we have a prime example of such a work. Aquinas does not attempt to prove what lies beyond the province or power of reason to establish; nor does he ever refrain from using his reason to think about mysteries of faith, such as the Trinity and the Incarnation, that are beyond the power of reason ever fully to comprehend.

Nevertheless, when Aquinas comes to the treatment of angels in the *Summa*, he fails to distinguish between those questions that arise for the dogmatic theologian in the light of revelation and those that a philosopher, considering angels as objects of thought and as a possible mode of being, would undertake to answer without any reference whatsoever to revelation, to declared dogmas, or articles of religious faith. If, as a dogmatic and yet speculative theologian, he had restricted himself to those questions that properly belong to his discipline and had avoided questions that are purely philosophical, his treatment of angels in the *Summa* would have been much less extensive. He would also have omitted certain matters that neither have a basis in revelation nor demand the attention of reason.

What I have just said about the treatment of angels by Aquinas accords with the comments of modern theologians, both Catholic and Protestant, who in one mood or another, sympathetic or adverse, regard his angelology as overblown.

For example, the great Catholic scholar, Étienne Gilson, a leading twentieth-century exponent of Thomistic thought, tells us that "the Thomistic angelology does not constitute in the mind of its author an inquiry of a specifically theological kind"; and he goes on to explain that it is "the final stage of a slow evolution of ideas, in the course of which heterogeneous elements converged, some of strictly religious, some of purely philosophical origin."

The most recent English translation of the *Summa Theologica*, the Blackfriars edition produced by the Dominicans under the general editorship of Father Thomas Gilby, contains commentaries on the work in its Introductions, and in a number of appendices.

In the appendix dealing with "Angelology in the Church and in St. Thomas," it is pointed out that the official doctrine of the church concerning angels is much more restricted or reticent than the speculative treatment of them in the *Summa*. Calling it "the most brilliant piece of speculation on the subject produced by a Western theologian," the writer of the appendix adds that it also "summarizes and critically assesses the theological tradition on the matter." That tradition, "formed chiefly by three writers, Dionysius, Augustine, and Gregory the Great, derived its essential data from Scripture," but it "inevitably derived much also from the assumptions and preoccupations . . . of the culture in which it was born and grew up."

That same appendix quotes criticisms levelled by a contemporary Catholic theologian, Karl Rahner, against the excesses of Patristic and mediaeval angelology. These include the charge that mediaeval theologians, Aquinas among them, yielded to "a tendency to turn angelology virtually into a pretext for metaphysical rather than properly theological investigations."

In one of their Introductions, the editors of the Blackfriars edition call attention to the fact that in twentieth-century theology, especially in the trend responsive to the demythologizing protocols of Rudolf Bultmann, angels "have had a rather bad press" and "for a good many modern theologians they are either to be 'demythologized' out of existence or given a purely symbolic interpretation." Giving angels a purely symbolic interpretation, I must point out in passing, is of much earlier origin, making its appearance in the *Leviathan* of Thomas Hobbes in the seventeenth century.

A century earlier than Hobbes, the great Protestant reformer, John Calvin, in his *Institutes of the Christian Religion*, sternly repudiated "that nugatory philosophy concerning the holy angels, which teaches that they are nothing but inspirations or good motivations by God in the minds of men." In Calvin's view, the testimonies of Scripture concerning the reality of angels requires us to reject the notion that they are merely symbolic—visions or voices experienced by men.

At the same time, Calvin enjoins us "not to speak, or think, or even desire to know, concerning obscure subjects, anything beyond the information given us in the Divine word." He cautions us, in reading Scripture, "to investigate and meditate upon things conducive to edification; not to indulge curiosity or the study of things unprofitable." Following his own rules for theologizing, his treatment of angels is therefore much less extensive than that of Aquinas, eliminating all questions that he regards as philosophical because they do not arise from the consideration of scriptural texts.

It is possible to go too far in the direction prescribed by Calvin. Karl Barth, a leading twentieth-century follower of Calvin, allows himself to be driven to the opposite extreme by his rejection of the excessively philosophical approach of Aquinas. He regards this as uncalled for by the task of dogmatic theology, or what he calls "church dogmatics."

In his judgment, Aquinas' angelology "offers us a classical example of how not to proceed in this matter. . . . In the matter of angels it is better to look resolutely and exclusively in a different direction than to try to look at the Bible and other sources of knowledge at one and the same time." If we do that, "our philosophy will spoil our theology, and our theology our philosophy."

In Barth's view, "Holy Scripture gives us quite enough to think of regarding angels." They are, for the most part, represented there as the messengers sent by God to man to announce his intentions or to manifest his presence. This is the revealed fact upon which theology should concentrate its attention when faith seeks understanding.

Scripture tells us nothing about many matters that are the substance of questions treated in the angelology of Aquinas. These, including the existence, nature, and properties of angels as purely spiritual beings, incorporeal substances, minds without bodies, belong to philosophy, not to theology.

The acceptance of Barth's extreme position with regard to the narrow confines of an angelology that restricts itself to scriptural revelation concerning them leads to a number of unfortunate consequences.

In the first place, it provides no protection against a purely literal or fundamentalist reading of the Bible which would lead us to believe that angels have actual bodies with two or more pairs of wings and that they have these bodies both when they dwell in heaven and when they come to earth.

In the second place, suppose we make no attempt to give reasons for thinking that purely spiritual beings really exist and that the angels who make their appearance on earth, either with the winged bodies they assume for the purpose or in human form, are identical with the pure spirits or unembodied intellects that constitute the heavenly host. What defense, then, can be erected against the position taken by Thomas Hobbes in the seventeenth century, and in our own time by Rudolf Bultmann and many other moderns who follow him?

Angels may appear to men in various guises, as they are so described in the Bible; but why cannot these apparitions be interpreted as visionary visitations of the same sort that human beings have when they are dreaming? Why cannot all the references to angels in Holy Scripture be interpreted symbolically as manifesting God's presence rather than literally as representing the presence of God's messengers—members of the heavenly host come to earth in bodily form?

Calvin and, after him, Barth, reject the answer given to these questions by Hobbes and Bultmann, but neither of them, in their too-restricted theology, can give reasons for supporting that rejection—reasons to be found in the less restricted theology of Aquinas. They make the mistake of thinking that any reasoning about the real existence, nature, properties, and actions of angels as spiritual beings must be philosophical because it goes beyond the consideration of angels as God's messengers to man. It is philosophical, but it is philosophy in the service of theology, not philosophy concerned with examining the consequences of the hypothesis that minds can exist without bodies—a possibility to be explored.

How, then, shall we draw the line, not drawn at all by Aquinas and drawn too rigidly by Calvin and Barth—the line dividing those questions about angels that belong to dogmatic theology from those that belong to speculative philosophy?

Appropriate exclusively to theology are questions raised by scriptural texts that require some interpretation beyond what is literally said in Sacred Scripture and that may, therefore, require philosophical analysis and reasoning to answer. In addition, there may be questions about angels that would not and could not be raised except within the context of religious beliefs or dogmas about other matters. These, too, belong exclusively to dogmatic theology even though they cannot be answered without recourse to philosophical thought.

What is left over? Any and every question about angels that stems from an initial and purely philosophical hypothesis; namely, that purely spiritual beings—minds without bodies—are a metaphysical possibility. Such thinking about angels proceeds without any reference whatsoever to Divine revelation, Sacred Scriptures, religious dogmas or beliefs. It draws no aid or direction from the light of faith.

The division just made between questions for the theologians and questions for the philosopher (when he functions outside the context of theology) corresponds to the division in this book between matters to be treated in Part Two and matters to be treated in Part Three. In Part Two, we shall be concerned with angels as objects of religious belief. In Part Three, we shall be concerned with angels as objects of philosophical thought.

Part Four, the most important part of this book with respect to the philosophical significance that angels have for us, is concerned with angelistic fallacies in modern thought. A sound assessment of human nature and of man's place in the cosmic scheme cannot be achieved without detecting these fallacies and correcting them. That is why a philosophical consideration of angels, even if they do not exist, is of such critical significance.

PART TWO

Angels as Objects of Religious Belief

3

The Dogma and the Doctrines

(1) Why a Belief in Angels?

WHY should religious Jews, Christians, and Muslims believe in angels? And when they do believe, what is it that they believe?

It may not be true that all of the faithful in these three religious communities acknowledge the belief in question or are even aware that their religious commitment includes that article of faith. For the rest, whose religious faith implicitly or explicitly involves a belief in angels, that belief may simply express an espousal of the official creed of the religious community to which they belong. It is questionable whether many of them have given much, if any, thought to this act of faith on their part.

Thinking about it must start with the question why a belief in angels has become a dogma or a declaration of faith in the three great Western religions that still prosper in the world in their orthodox forms. The answer lies in the first and fundamental article of faith that is common to all three religions.

All three, often referred to as religions of the book, are distinguished by their faith in certain writings as Sacred Scriptures because they are the revealed word of God—for Jews, the Old Testament; for Christians, the Old Testament and the New; for Muslims, the Old Testament and the Koran. The assertion that these writings contain Divine revelation is an affirmation that is both unprovable and irrefutable. It does not belong, therefore, in the domain of historical, scientific, or philosophical knowledge. It belongs to the realm of religious belief.

Beginning with what I have called the first and most fundamental article of faith, all further religious beliefs or articles of
faith are derived by a process of exegesis or interpretation of
whatever texts each of the three religions has come to regard as
canonical, not apocryphal. These additional articles of faith may
be promulgated as dogmas or they may be set forth in some
formal declaration of a creed to which the faithful are expected
to assent.

Dogmatic theology, which is sometimes called sacred theology
or sacred doctrine, carries the process of interpretation one step
further. Starting from the promulgated dogmas or credal declarations of one sort or another, theologians attempt to formulate
doctrines that provide some elaboration and explication of the
articles of faith. Theological doctrines emerge from a process
that has been referred to as faith seeking understanding.

Though theological doctrines develop within a framework that
is imposed by dogmas or creeds, their formulation does not depend solely upon the canonical sources from which the dogmas
or creeds are derived. All human knowledge is grist to the mill
of the theologian.

Whatever is known at a given time, whatever philosophical
theories or insights are germane, can be employed by the theologian in his effort to eke out an understanding that aims to
render religious beliefs more intelligible to the minds of those
who espouse them. The theologian can also attempt to defend or
uphold these beliefs by showing that they are not unreasonable,
even though reason is unable to provide them with such adequate support that it would then become unnecessary to affirm
them by an act of faith.

These things being so, we must look to passages in Sacred
Scriptures in order to discover the basis for the religious belief
in angels. In doing so, we must, of course, confine ourselves to
the canonical texts. This eliminates the apocryphal books of the
Bible in which, by the way, there are statements about angels
that have exercised considerable influence on subsequent speculations about them. It also eliminates a vast variety of post-

scriptural writings that have become, in varying degrees, authoritative in the Jewish, Christian, and Islamic traditions.

The reason for their exclusion from our present inquiry is that the many highly fanciful conjectures about angels that emerged from these writings go far beyond the sober beliefs that have their foundation or warranty in canonical texts.

In the Jewish tradition, this applies to much that is said about angels in Talmudic and Midrashic literature, as well as in the even more extravagant angelic legends and lore, fantasies and fictions, to be found in the writings of the Essenes, the Gnostics, the Cabalists, and in the mystical writings of the Hasidim.

In the Christian tradition, it applies to a sixth-century work, *The Celestial Hierarchy,* supposedly written by a monk from Syria who bears the name of Dionysius, and who has been called the pseudo-Areopagite because legend has it that he was converted to Christianity by St. Paul, on the Areopagus in Athens. In the later Middle Ages, his treatise on angels achieved unquestionable authority, and Dionysius or St. Denis was venerated as the first bishop and patron of Paris. This has been completely discredited by modern scholarship. Modern theologians, both Catholic and Protestant, no longer regard *The Celestial Hierarchy* as being an authoritative source for theological doctrines concerning angels.

Anyone who wishes to become acquainted with the legends and lore, the extravaganzas, fantasies, and fictions about angels can do so by going to Gustav Davidson's *A Dictionary of Angels,* in which the bibliography of books about angels, most of them nontheological and nonphilosophical, takes up twenty-four pages. Another book of similar source material, profusely illustrated, is *Angels* by Peter Lamborn Wilson. Both books are in print.

(2) *What the Belief Is*

So far I have answered only the first of the questions with which this chapter began. The second question, the more difficult of the two, remains to be answered. When religious Jews,

Christians, and Muslims believe in angels, what is it that they believe and why?

If the scriptural texts on which the belief in angels rests were exclusively narrative passages in which angels appeared to human beings either in ordinary human guise or in the corporeal form of winged figures, effulgent with dazzling light and with haloes around their heads, and if these passages were given a strictly literal reading, the ensuing belief in angels would hardly be a belief in the existence of purely spiritual beings—unembodied intelligences, minds without bodies.

The objects believed to have real existence would have to be considered as included among God's creatures in the corporeal world, however strange that belief would then become, not only in terms of all the knowledge we have concerning the natural world of physical things, but also because they are not mentioned in *Genesis* as included among God's corporeal creatures.

What has prevented so strange a belief from having been adopted? Three things to be found in Sacred Scriptures have been interpreted in a way that crucially defines the religious belief in angels and makes that belief much less bizarre.

First, scriptural exegesis must and does take account of all the passages in which angels are spoken of as messengers from God to mankind. Coming to earth, bearing messages to man from God, where do they come from? From heaven which is God's dwelling place. Is that a physical place inhabited by bodies? The angels assume bodies of one sort or another when they come to earth, but when they are in heaven, they must be bodiless.

Second, scriptural exegesis must and does take account of those scriptural passages in which angels are referred to as members of a heavenly host, as surrounding the throne of God in heaven, as belonging to the company of heaven. Though these passages are much less numerous than the narrative passages already mentioned, they cannot be overlooked.

Third, and most important of all, is the scriptural exegesis that overcomes the obstacle to believing in angels as purely spiritual beings. That obstacle lies in a question that must be answered. Why does not the first chapter of *Genesis* mention the angels as God's spiritual creatures before it proceeds with the enumeration of God's corporeal creatures? The question is answered by the brilliant interpretation given the opening sentence of *Genesis* by St. Augustine.

"In the beginning God created heaven and earth." If, in that sentence, the word "heaven" is interpreted as signifying the corporeal heaven occupied by celestial bodies, such as stars and planets, then the interpretation is contradicted by the fact that in subsequent sentences of *Genesis* 1, the physical firmament and light come into being—after, not simultaneously with, the heaven that God created along with the earth.

According to Augustine, the most fitting interpretation of the opening sentence is one that reads the word "heaven" as signifying the whole realm of spiritual creatures and the word "earth" as signifying the whole material creation, the realm of corporeal things, including the visible firmament with its stars and planets.

That interpretation is confirmed by other uses of the word "heaven" in the literature and liturgies of the Western religions. When, in the Lord's Prayer, the supplicant says "Our Father which art in heaven, hallowed be Thy name . . . Thy will be done, on earth as it is in heaven," the sovereignty of God over this planet, over the solar system, over our galaxy, and over all the galaxies there are can hardly be what is intended. On the contrary, the sense of the statement must be that God's will prevails in the realm of bodies as it does in the realm of spirits.

Similar interpretations of the word "heaven" as signifying the realm of spiritual creatures must be accorded such phrases as "with angels, archangels, and all the company of heaven," "the heavenly host," and "the kingdom of heaven." Heaven being the dwelling place of God, preeminently a purely spiritual being, it cannot be regarded as a physical place, a space that can be occupied by bodies. It is not out there or up there or anywhere that has a location in the physical cosmos.

All this comes to a head in the interpretation we must put upon the opening sentence of the Nicene Creed: "I believe in one God, Father Almighty, Maker of heaven and earth, And of all things visible and invisible."

The maker of earth (which stands for the whole physical cosmos) is the creator of all things visible—either perceptible by the senses or detectible by means of sensitive instruments.

The maker of heaven (which stands for the realm of spiritual beings) is the creator of all things invisible—neither perceptible nor detectible in any way because they are totally immaterial.

Like the words "heaven" and "earth," the words "visible" and "invisible" cannot be read with their customary meanings, according to which air and sound are invisible, but certainly not imperceptible or physically undetectible.

As contrasted with the visible, the invisible refers to everything that lies beyond the reach of sense-perception or physical detection, because it is totally nonphysical—immaterial or incorporeal. Only purely spiritual beings are invisible in this sense of the word. As Karl Barth points out, heaven "in distinction from earth, exists as invisible creaturely reality."

While the Nicene Creed is a declaration of pre-Reformation Christian beliefs, there is nothing in its opening statement from which Protestant reformers would dissent; nor would any Protestant sect that has arisen since the Reformation find in it any grounds for objection, as might be the case with other avowals that come later in the creed. The same can be said, without qualification, for the orthodox churches of the Eastern, Greek, or Russian rite; and even for orthodox religious Jews and Muslims.

In short, in that first clause of the creed, we have the dogma that purely spiritual creatures have been created by God. When that dogma, shared by orthodox Judaism, by all, or certainly most, branches and sects of Christianity, and by the two main sects of Islam, is illuminated by the scriptural passages in which some of those spiritual creatures come from heaven to earth as angels—as messengers from God to man—the spiritual beings believed in by religious Jews, Christians, and Muslims are at once seen to differ radically from what at first might appear to be their anticipations in Greek and Hellenistic philosophy.

The intelligences or secondary unmoved movers that function as celestial motors in Aristotle's cosmology are neither created by Aristotle's God nor serve Aristotle's God as messengers to mankind. They may be minds without bodies but they are neither spiritual *creatures* nor do they function *angelically* in an intermediary role between God in heaven and man on earth.

The same fundamental differences will be found between the angelic spiritual creatures believed in by religious Jews, Christians, and Muslims and the intelligences that are below God and above man in the neo-Platonic cosmologies of Plotinus and Proclus during the Hellenistic period.

These critical differences, it should be observed, were noted by the Hellenistic Jewish philosopher, Philo, and by the mediaeval Jewish theologian, Moses Maimonides, as well as by the great Catholic theologians of the twelfth and thirteenth century—Albert the Great, Thomas Aquinas, and Bonaventure.

In the Muslim community, the two greatest of Islam's philosophers differ on this point, Avicenna being unwilling and Averroës willing to identify the angels who make their appearance in the Old Testament and the Koran, and are also God's spiritual creatures, with the intelligences posited in Aristotle's cosmology.

Aristotle's uncreated and unembodied intelligences function exclusively as causes of motion in the material heavens—the celestial spheres of the physical universe. They may be spiritual beings, but they are not God's *creatures*, they are not God's *messengers*, and so they are not angels.

(3) *From Dogma to Doctrines*

The creed formulated at the Council of Nicaea in 325 declared God to be the maker of all things visible and invisible. The earlier Apostle's Creed mentioned only "heaven and earth." It was the Nicene Creed that combined the two dichotomies and implied that these two district realms of God's created universe were, on the one hand, heaven and all things invisible and, on the other hand, earth and all things visible.

It was not until the year 1215—about fifty years before Thomas Aquinas wrote his two great theological summations in which an elaborate doctrine of angels was set forth—that the Fourth Lateran Council made explicit all the implications of the first sentence of *Genesis*, so eloquently and cogently expounded by St. Augustine in Book XII of his *Confessions*.

The Fourth Lateran Council declared that God is

creator of all things visible and invisible, spiritual and corporeal; who by his almighty power, together at the beginning of time, formed out of nothing the spiritual creature and the corporeal creature, that is, the angelic and the terrestrial; and then the human creature, composed of both body and spirit. For Satan and the other devils were created by God, and created good in nature; it is of themselves they have become evil.

From my reading of Martin Luther's *Table Talk* and John Calvin's *Institutes of the Christian Religion*, I would venture to say that the two great Protestant reformers would find nothing in this dogmatic declaration to challenge, not even the last sentence that might prove troublesome to later Protestant theologians. I would also say the same thing about the great theologians of orthodox Judaism, again with the possible exception of the last sentence about the creation and the fall of Satan.

I do not mean to imply that in the modern development of Protestant theology, no dissenters can be found. In the nineteenth century, Carl Hase in a book entitled *Gnosis*, published in 1827, regarded the reality of spiritual creatures as highly problematical; and David F. Strauss a little later, in 1840, maintained that when humanity "freed itself from the Middle Ages," and adopted a quite different set of principles "the notion of angels which had flourished on very different soil was bound to wither away on this alien territory." Still later, in our own century, Rudolf Bultmann dismissed them from the realm of religious belief as nothing but antiquated myths or fictions.

Still another dissident view was expressed by Friedrich Schleiermacher in the nineteenth century. Though, in his view, the notion of angels "neither contains anything impossible nor contradicts the basis of all God-fearing consciousness," Schleiermacher was unwilling to concede anything more than that the mention of angels "can be present in the language of Christianity without imposing any necessary affirmations" concerning their reality. His followers echoed his views, saying, as Spinner did, that "the reality of angels is questionable; their influence none"; or declaring, as Kaftan did, that "angels are not an object of faith."

Nevertheless, as Karl Barth points out, Schleiermacher and his followers did not, like Strauss and Bultmann, explicitly deny the existence of angels. They were, in Barth's opinion, deterred from doing so by the many scriptural references to angels that they were unable to dismiss as out of place in God's revelation about the universe He created.

The references to angels in Sacred Scriptures did not prevent the aristocratic Sadduccees in ancient Israel from denying their existence, as we learn from St. Paul in *Acts* 23–68. But this denial did not prevail in later Jewish religious thought. On the contrary, as has already been noted, post-exilic Judaism moved in the very opposite direction, not only affirming the existence of angels but also conjuring up fantastic notions about angels that went far beyond what scriptural references warranted.

In the Christian tradition, there were also early doubters or deniers. Origen, for example, questioned whether incorporeality can be attributed to any being except God; and Gregory of Nazianzus found it difficult to find the right words in which to speak about angels. But after the Nicene declaration at the time of Augustine, and in the light of the foundations he laid for both Catholic and Protestant theology, there are few, if any, naysayers in the Christian tradition until we come to modern times.

In a long line that leads from Pope Gregory the Great in the sixth century, John Scotus Erigena in the ninth century, and St. Anselm, Archbishop of Canterbury in the eleventh century, to

St. Albert the Great, St. Thomas Aquinas, and St. Bonaventure
in the twelfth and thirteenth centuries, the yea-sayers prevailed
and developed a variety of theological doctrines about angels,
their heavenly life, their earthly visitations, and their division
into the good and bad angels, the angels of heaven and hell.

From the title of this section, it may have been noticed by
readers that the religious dogma concerning angels is singular,
but that the theological doctrines are plural. While Aquinas and
Bonaventure subscribe to the same dogma, as formulated by the
Fourth Lateran Council, they differ in their angelologies on a
variety of points, many of them minor. So, too, while Calvin
would not quarrel with the Lateran declaration, his theological
handling of the subject not only differs from the treatment given
it by Aquinas and Bonaventure, but is also much less extensive.
He limits himself to "what the Lord has been pleased for us to
know concerning his angels," as that is revealed to us in Sacred
Scriptures.

This raises a problem about how far it is appropriate for theologians to ask and attempt to answer questions about angels.
The solution of that problem would seem to be: no farther than
is necessary to understand angels as objects of religious belief,
based on the interpretation of Sacred Scriptures.

To say, as Karl Barth does, that the realm of heaven and the
incorporeal creatures who dwell there are not only invisible, but
also incomprehensible to us, limits the consideration of angels
too severely. The incorporeal and the invisible may be unimag-
inable by us, but they are not unthinkable or unintelligible. Angels are no more incomprehensible than minds or intellects are,
whether embodied or not.

God, heaven, and purely spiritual beings are certainly beyond
imagining, but they are not beyond our power to grasp by
thought, in the same way that by taking thought we can reflexively understand our own minds.

The development of theological doctrines concerning angels
must have recourse to intellectual reflection if the aim of the

dogmatic theologian is to be realized. How else can faith seek understanding? In what other way can what is believed by the faithful be rendered intelligible and defended as reasonable?

The only limitation on this effort must come from two cautious restraints: first, not to try to understand what is truly incomprehensible by us—the great religious mysteries; and second, not to develop theological doctrines about matters that lie outside the framework of scripturally based beliefs. To do so is to engage in extraneous embellishments and elaborations of doctrine.

In the chapters of Part Two that follow I am going to deal with questions about angels that fall well within the limitations just mentioned. All will be questions that belong to dogmatic theology concerning the reality, nature, attributes, and actions of angels, not philosophical questions that can be raised without any regard whatsoever to scripturally based religious beliefs. I will refrain from raising the latter until Part Three.

In attempting to expound a theological doctrine about angels, I will take as my model and guide the angelology of Thomas Aquinas as that is set forth in his Treatise on Angels in the *Summa Theologica*, drawing also on his discussion of angels in other of his writings. Wherever it seems fitting and proper, I will call attention to points on which other theologians differ, in order to remind readers that, while there may be only one dogma about angels, there are many doctrines.

In the exposition that follows in Chapters 4, 5, and 6, I will omit the discussion of the three hierarchies and nine orders of angels that Aquinas discusses at such great length in Question 108 of his Treatise on the Divine Government. This discussion draws almost entirely on the authority of *The Celestial Hierarchy* by Dionysius the Pseudo-Areopagite, not on what is said about different kinds and grades of angels in Sacred Scriptures. The whole discussion of these matters in Question 108 of the *Summa Theologica* is, therefore, to be regarded as an extraneous embellishment and elaboration of theological theorizing about angels.

(4) *An Angelic Entertainment*

In lecturing about angels to a variety of audiences, I have found that the ordering of the angels together with the naming of their ranks in the scale of spiritual beings arouses interest equal to or exceeding interest in the question about the number of angels on the head of a pin. Once that question is answered, the interest dies; but the hierarchical organization of the heavenly society sustains its fascination for the intellectual imagination. In addition, I have found that it proves to be highly entertaining to almost everyone who learns about the scheme of things in Heaven.

Though what is to be learned on this score is neither scripturally-based theological doctrine nor a philosophically reasoned explanation of how angels, as spiritual creatures, stand in relation to one another, the entertainment afforded by the organization chart justifies a brief account of it here before we go on to more serious doctrinal consideration in the chapters to follow.

Before Dionysius wrote his *Celestial Hierarchy* early in the sixth century, the grouping of the angels in different classes and the ranking of these classes in a descending scale of perfection had been discussed by theologians. In the Patristic period, St. Augustine had refrained from being definite about the angelic order, but St. Jerome and St. Ambrose had constructed lists that included the following named ranks: seraphim, cherubim, thrones, dominations (or dominions), virtues, powers, principalities, archangels, and angels.

The word "angel," of course, is the generic name for all members of the heavenly host, as well as the name assigned to the lowest rank in the descending scale of spiritual creatures. All of these names make their appearance in Sacred Scriptures, four of them quite frequently ("seraphim," "cherubim," "archangels," and "angels") and the rest much less frequently. But nowhere in Sacred Scriptures do the nine names appear *in any one place;* nor are the different types of angels thus named ever ordered *in one fixed scheme* of organization. Some scriptural passages read as if archangels were the highest echelon; some assign seraphim to that place; and sometimes such phrases as "angel of the Lord" and "angels of the throne" seem to indicate the spiritual elite.

Beginning with Dionysius and in the writings of subsequent theologians who accept his work as authoritative, the organization chart became almost canonical. The society or community of angels was divided into three hierarchies and in each hierarchy there were three choirs or orders of angels; in the first and topmost hierarchy, seraphim, cherubim, and thrones in descending order; in the second and middle hierarchy, dominions, virtues, and powers; in the third and bottom hierarchy, principalities, archangels, and angels.

Expressed in the simplest terms, the descending order of the hierarchies, and of the three choirs in each hierarchy, consists in grades of creaturely perfection—the seraphim representing the highest grade of perfection among God's creatures, and mere angels, the lowest. The perfection referred to is not moral, but metaphysical—a perfection in mode of being, in the created nature of the being.

The descending order can also be understood in terms of proximity to or remoteness from God, the creative source of all beings, spiritual and corporeal. The ranking of the seraphim as supreme among created beings places them nearest to God, with archangels and mere angels occupying places furthest away.

Gradations of perfection or excellence in being and degrees of proximity to God in the spiritual realm have consequences for spiritual life and action at these different levels.

Spinning out these consequences in extraordinary detail constituted the fabric of *The Celestial Hierarchy*, a speculative innovation by Dionysius that gained increasing authority in the centuries that followed, first through its acceptance by Pope Gregory the Great, then through its repetition by Scotus Erigena, and finally through its adoption and reworking by Albert the Great, Thomas Aquinas, and Bonaventure in the twelfth and thirteenth centuries.

It may be wondered how Dionysius came to have such authority for his mediaeval successors, an authority almost equal to that of the Bible. As good an explanation as any is one that Étienne Gilson attributes to Bonaventure, who thought that a special revelation about the angelic orders had been received by St. John the Evangelist and by St. Paul. Dionysius learned about this arcane matter from St. Paul, who instructed him at the time of his conversion. If this legend was generally current in the Middle Ages from the sixth century on, it explains the almost canonical authority of the writings of Dionysius.

Neither the authority nor the reputation of Dionysius prospered after the Protestant Reformation. In one brief reference to him, Calvin said:

No man can deny that great subtlety and acuteness is discovered by Dionysius, whoever he was, in many parts of his treatise on the Celestial Hierarchy; but if any one enters into a critical examination of it, he will find the greatest part of it to be mere babbling. . . . A reader of that book would suppose that the author was a man descended from heaven, giving an account of things that he had not learned from the information of others, but had seen with his own eyes. But Paul, who was "caught up to the third heaven," [2 Corinthians, xii, i] not only has told us no such things, but has even declared that it is not lawful for men to utter the sacred things which he had seen.

As a disciple of Calvin, Karl Barth dismisses the work of Dionysius even more summarily as "one of the greatest frauds in Church history." Nevertheless, Barth concedes that "this does not alter the fact that within its limits his work is one of those original and masterly ventures which do not often occur in the history of theology."

Either directly, or indirectly through its reworking by Aquinas, the Dionysian blueprint of the nine-storied structure of heaven was an architectural masterpiece that captured the imagination of the poets from Dante's *Divine Comedy* and Milton's *Paradise Lost* on. Not only the poets, but almost everyone else has been entranced and entertained by it.

These things being so, let us see how the matter is handled

by Aquinas, following the lead of his teacher Albert and relying heavily on the formative work of Dionysius. While remaining faithful to the substance of its source in Dionysius, the treatment given the subject by Aquinas represents a remarkable alteration in style.

Karl Barth, who is neither a disciple nor a defender of Thomas Aquinas, contrasts the two styles as follows: "The *Hierarchy* of Dionysius," he says, "reads more like a dithyramb" bombastic in language and filled with "garrulous obscurity or obscure garrulity." With the *Summa Theologica* of Aquinas, he writes,

we enter into the sphere of the most calm and sober enquiry, and teaching of the strictest method and of corresponding statement—a sphere where everything necessary and nothing unnecessary is said.

In concentrating attention on the Thomistic exposition of the matter, I do not mean to imply that his account of the angelic orders is the only one or the one that is right. There is no basis for according it such status, either on theological or philosophical grounds.

A fundamental difference of opinion existed between Aquinas and Bonaventure about the principles that generate the hierarchies and orders of angels. That difference is reported as follows by Étienne Gilson, the great historian of mediaeval thought:

In the teaching of St. Thomas Aquinas the angels are hierarchically ordered according to the exigencies of a principle which is as linear as possible: the increasing simplicity of the intelligible species [i.e., infused or innate ideas] by which they know. The order followed by St. Bonaventure, although no less real, is yet more complicated, for he employs many correspondences suggested to him by the principle of analogy. The angels are ordered in hierarchies according to the different states and degrees in which they are situated by the illumination which God bestows upon them.

Gilson leaves it at that and refrains, as he must, from arbitrating the difference or judging which view should prevail.

In the Treatise on the Divine Government in Part I of *Summa*

Theologica, Question 108, devoted to a consideration of "the array of angels," consists of eight articles, each posing a question: (1) "whether all the angels belong to one hierarchy," to which the answer is negative; (2) "whether in one hierarchy, there is just one order," to which the answer is also negative; (3)"whether within one order there are many angels," to which the answer is affirmative; (4)"whether the differentiation of hierarchies and orders comes from distinctions among angelic natures," to which the answer is again affirmative; (5)"whether the names of the different orders are properly assigned," to which the affirmative answer expresses approval of the names that Dionysius assigned to them, accompanied by argumentation in support of that approval; (6) whether, as the orders are compared with one another, their attributes or characteristics are properly described, to which once again the affirmative answer explicates and enlarges on the speculations of Dionysius.

I have omitted Articles 7 and 8, the one concerned with whether the angelic hierarchies and orders will persist after Judgment Day, the other with whether the souls of the saved are taken upon into the angelic orders and whether the communion of saints is joined with the society of angels, because these questions are not strictly germane to our present interest in the organization chart of the angelic realm.

Of the six questions that are germane, it is the sixth, taken together with much that is said in the preceding five, that sets forth the highly imaginative yet strictly analytical theory of the differences that put each of the three hierarchies in its proper place in the heavenly scheme and, within each hierarchy, each of its constituent choirs.

Some readers, I am sure, will now be satisfied with what they have been told so far. There may be others who find the whole subject so entertaining that they wish to learn more. For them, I cannot do better than quote in full the exposition of the theory of Thomas Aquinas by his most learned twentieth-century disciple, Étienne Gilson, from the English translation of whose book, *Le Thomisme*, the following passage is taken.

Any paraphrase of it, however managed, would produce an inferior version; excerpting would simply subtract what cannot be omitted without loss. Therefore, I will tamper with it only by breaking it up into shorter paragraphs for ease of reading and by adding bracketed words or phrases to explain certain terms that Gilson uses.

This innate possession of intelligible species [ideas] is common to all the angels and characteristic of their nature; but not all of them possess in themselves all the species, and hereon their distinction is based. The relative superiority of created beings is constituted by their greater or lesser proximity and resemblance to the one first being which is God.

Now, the whole plenitude of intellectual knowledge, possessed by God, is concentrated for Him in one point, namely the Divine essence in which God knows all things. This intellectual plenitude is to be found again in created intelligences, but in an inferior mode and with less simplicity; the intelligences inferior to God know therefore by many different means what God knows in one unique object, and the more subordinate the nature of a given intelligence is, the more numerous must be the means employed in knowing.

In short, the superiority of the angels increases in proportion as the number of species [ideas] required by them in order to apprehend the universe of intelligibles decreases.

We know, moreover, that, as regards the angels, each individual constitutes an original degree of being. The simplicity of knowledge is accordingly continually degraded and broken up in descending from the first angel to the last. Still, three distinct main stages may be observed in this series.

At the first stage are the angels who know the intelligible essences, inasmuch as they proceed from the first universal principle which is God. This mode of knowing pertains properly to the first hierarchy, ranged immediately round God, of which it may be said, with St. Dionysius, that it dwells within the vestibule of the Godhead.

At the second stage are the angels who know intelligibles in so far as they are subject to the most universal of created causes; this mode of knowing pertains to the second hierarchy.

Lastly, the third stage is occupied by the angels knowing intelligibles as applied to particular beings and dependent on particular causes; these angels constitute the third hierarchy.

There is consequently a decreasing generality and simplicity in the distribution of angelic knowledge; some, turned wholly to God, are concerned entirely with the contemplation within Him of intelligible essences; others contemplate them in the universal causes of creation, i.e., in a plurality of objects; others, lastly, consider them in the determinate form of particular effects, i.e., in a multiplicity of objects, equal to the number of created beings.

In defining in detail the mode according to which the separate intelligences [minds without bodies, i.e., angels] apprehend their object, we are led to observe three different orders within each hierarchy.

For it was said that the first hierarchy contemplates the intelligible essences within God Himself; now God is the end of all creatures; the angels of this hierarchy contemplate, therefore, as their peculiar object, the supreme end of the universe which is the goodness of God.

Those who apprehend it with the utmost clearness are called Seraphim, because they burn and are, as it were, aflame with love for that object of which they possess the most perfect knowledge.

The other angels of the first hierarchy contemplate Divine goodness, no longer directly and in itself, but according to the wisdom of Providence. They are called Cherubim, i.e., "plenitude of wisdom," because they have a clear vision of the first operating virtue of the Divine models of things.

Immediately below these are the angels who consider the disposition of Divine judgments; and as the throne is the symbol of judiciary power, they have received the name of Thrones. This does not mean that the goodness of God, His essence and His knowledge by which He knows the disposition of beings, are in Him three distinct things; they are simply three aspects under which finite intelligences, such as the angels, are able to envisage His perfect simplicity.

The second hierarchy knows the reason of things, not in God Himself as in a single object, but in the plurality of universal causes: its proper object is therefore the general ordering of means in view of the end.

Now this universal ordering of things presupposes the existence of many ordering minds: these are the Dominations [also called Dominions] whose name signifies authority, because they order what others are to execute. The general directions given by these angels are received by others, multiplying and distributing them according to the diverse effect to be produced.

These latter angels have the name of Virtues, because they impart to the general causes the necessary energy to preserve them from failure in the accomplishment of their numerous operations. This order therefore presides over the operations of the entire universe, and we may therefore reasonably ascribe to it the movement of the celestial bodies, as the universal causes whereby all the particular effects in nature are produced. It falls also within the province of these angels to carry out the Divine effects which interrupt the ordinary course of nature and are usually in direct dependance on the stars.

Lastly, the universal order of Providence, already existing in its effects, is preserved from all confusion by the Powers whose office it is to protect it against all evil influences likely to disturb it.

With this last class of angels we reach the third hierarchy which knows the order of Divine Providence no longer in itself, nor in the general causes, but insofar as it is knowable in the multiplicity of particular causes. These angels are therefore directly charged with the ordering of human affairs.

Some of them are particularly concerned with the common and general good of nations and cities: on account of this position, they have been given the name of Principalities. The distinction of kingdoms, the passing of a temporal supremacy to this nation rather than to that, the conduct of princes and nobles, are matters of their direct competence.

Within that very general class of goods, there is one that concerns the individual taken in himself, but at the same time also a multitude of individual persons: these are the truths of Faith to be believed, and the Divine cult to be observed. The angels whose special objects are these goods, at the same time general and particular, bear the name of Archangels. It is they also who carry the most solemn messages entrusted to them by God to man: such was the Archangel Gabriel who came to announce the Incarnation of the Word, the only Son of God, the Truth which all men are bound to accept.

Lastly, we find a yet more particular good, which concerns each individual in himself and particularly. This order of good is in the hands of the Angels, strictly so called, the guardians of men and messengers of God to carry intimations of lesser importance. These Angels complete the inferior hierarchy of separate intelligences.

If anyone, contemplating this picture of the serried ranks of angels from the highest of the seraphim to the least of the guardian angels, wonders about the justice of the Divine plan that distributes God's favors so unequally, the resolving insight lies in the explanation that Piccarda gives Dante in the *Paradiso*.

Dante asks her if she is not discontented with her place in the lowest circle of heaven. Does she not wish to move up closer to the throne of God and enhance her participation in the beatific vision?

Piccarda answers by saying that no one in heaven is dissatisfied with the place assigned them, explaining to Dante that

From seat to seat throughout this realm, to all the realm is pleasing . . . for in His will our hearts have found their peace.

"Then it was clear to me," Dante adds, "that everywhere in Heaven is Paradise, even if the grace of God does not rain down in equal measure on all alike."

4

The Reality of Angels

(1) Why Try to Prove the Existence of Angels?

GOOD question. Why, indeed, since the religious belief in the
reality of angels has a secure foundation in Sacred Scriptures
accepted as Divine revelation? What can any argument devised
by reason add to the certainty faith claims for itself on the authority of God as its source and guarantee?

To be sure that the problem is clear, let me recapitulate the
steps taken in the preceding chapter to show how angels became
objects of religious belief and what that belief consisted in.

1. Sacred Scriptures, in many passages, attest the existence of
angels on earth, performing their mission as messengers from
God. In all of these earthly visitations, angels are described as
having some corporeal form or guise. They are not just voices
heard from an unseen source.

2. The account of creation in *Genesis* 1, with the word
"heaven" in the opening sentence interpreted in a way that seems
to be required by the sentences that follow, attests the existence
of an incorporeal realm of things invisible as well as the existence of the visible, material world in which we dwell.

3. Since angels, regardless of the corporeal forms or guises
that they assume in their earthly visitations, do not by their nature belong to the material world, and since, in coming from
God to man, they come from Heaven to earth, the scripturally
based religious belief in angels is a belief in the existence of purely
spiritual beings.

The third step, following inexorably from the first two, leads to the dogmatic or credal declaration of the reality of angels as an article of religious faith. Why, then, is there any need for a rationally developed argument in support of faith?

Faith does not need such support from reason to make it more secure or to increase the assurance with which it is held. It does not need it with regard to the existence of the God believed in by the faithful. Implicit in the first act of faith, which is a belief in Sacred Scriptures as Divine revelation, is belief in the deity who is the source of that revelation. What holds for God would seem to hold for God's angels.

Some dogmatic theologians (as, for example, Karl Barth and others who are of similar persuasion) reject all efforts to prove or argue for what is asserted by articles of faith on the ground that it is not necessary. They also think it is inappropriate in dogmatic theology, which, in their view, should entirely eschew philosophical reasoning.

Others think differently. Moses Maimonides, for example, in his *Guide for the Perplexed*, was one of the first of the mediaeval theologians to adapt philosophical arguments from Aristotle's *Physics* and *Metaphysics* and turn them into arguments for the existence of the Old Testament God. Nevertheless, this same Maimonides expressed the opinion that there was no need to prove the existence of angels, because belief in their reality has so firm a foundation in the Bible. There is an apparent inconsistency here that is difficult to understand.

However, most theologians in the Middle Ages—Arabic, Jewish, and Christian—and most Christian theologians since then do not agree with Karl Barth about rational arguments for God's existence. In their view, dogmatic theology involves more than a first step—an interpretation of Sacred Scriptures that defines what is to be believed on the basis of Divine revelation. It involves a second step—an attempt by reason to render intelligible what is believed and to defend it as not unreasonable.

The first step is indispensable and required; the second, dispensable but permissible. It is even desirable for the enhancement of faith. Without the second step, dogmatic theology is insufficiently speculative. It does not make the fullest use of the mind God gave mankind to understand His revelation and to defend the faith that rests on it.

Barth, in my judgment, is wrong in his over-zealous strictures against philosophical reasoning in dogmatic theology. Maimonides, it seems to me, is also wrong in admitting a place in theology for arguments with regard to God's existence, but conceding none to reasoning with regard to angels.

The one—certainly, the main—line of reasoning that bears on the existence of a realm of created spiritual beings was first developed by dogmatic theologians in the thirteenth century, notably Aquinas and Bonaventure. It was subsequently revived in relatively unaltered form by Locke and other philosophers in the seventeenth and eighteenth centuries.

Four things must be said about this argument. To state them is one thing; to explain them, another. The statements follow. The explanation will be found in the remainder of this chapter.

First, the line of reasoning referred to cannot be regarded as a purely philosophical argument because it rests on a theological premise that only faith can supply.

Second, while not purely philosophical, it presupposes an affirmation that only philosophical reasoning can support; namely, the possibility of angels.

Third, it does not succeed in demonstrating—proving, in the strict sense of that term—the existence of angels.

Fourth, it does succeed, nevertheless, in defending the religious belief in angels against those who dismiss such belief as unreasonable, preposterous, or absurd.

(2) *The Reason God Created Angels*

Any argument, scientific or philosophical, that attempts to establish the existence of something that is not immediately evident to sense perception must take the form of positing the existence of a cause that is needed to explain observed phenom-

ena or to explain the existence of something that is already known
to exist.

The only justification for affirming the existence of something
unperceived and, perhaps, imperceptible is that whatever it is
that needs to be explained cannot be explained in any other way.
This is the sound rule laid down by William of Ockham in the
fourteenth century and it has been followed ever since by careful, cautious scientists and philosophers.

The reasoning of nuclear physicists concerning the existence
of certain elementary particles that are intrinsically imperceptible takes this form. So, too, does a valid argument for the existence of God.

No similar form of argument is available with regard to the
existence of angels. There are no observed phenomena (exclud-
ing, of course, experiences reported in Sacred Scriptures) that
cannot be explained unless we affirm that angels exist and engage in certain causal actions. Nothing known by us to exist has
an existence that is inexplicable unless it is understood as an
effect of angelic action.

What is often miscalled an argument for the existence of angels amounts to nothing more than an effort to explain why God
included them in his creation of the universe. Why, in addition
to creating the whole physical cosmos and all the corporeal things
that constitute it, did God also create a realm of purely spiritual
beings—intelligences or minds without bodies?

If rational reflection can provide the explanation, it not only
enhances the religious belief in angels by rendering it intelligible. It also defends such a belief as reasonable against those who
scoff at it as absurd or preposterous.

The explanation advanced by Thomas Aquinas rests on a single insight. In his Treatise on Angels in the *Summa Theologica*,
answering the question whether there are entirely spiritual or
incorporeal creatures, Aquinas asserts that "the universe would
be incomplete without [them]."

In another treatise on the same subject, Aquinas further explains that the reason why God created angels is "the perfection

of the universe." To have perfection, "it must not lack any nature that can possibly exist."

Aquinas then adds a second reason. The perfection of the universe not only requires the existence of every kind of thing that is possible. It also requires an orderly arrangement of the things that constitute the aggregate of created substances.

An orderly arrangement would not be present if there were unfilled gaps in the scale of beings. "At the topmost summit of things there is a being which is in every way simple and one; namely, God." Therefore, Aquinas argues, corporeal things cannot·be "located immediately below God, for they are composite and divisible." That is why "one must posit many intermediates, through which we must come down from the highest point of the Divine simplicity to corporeal multiplicity."

Angels, being incorporeal and, therefore, having the simplicity that belongs to anything indivisible, occupy places in the scale of beings between God and man. This completes the picture.

The orderly arrangement that Aquinas thinks must characterize any universe created by God involves an ascending scale of beings from (1) inanimate and mindless physical things to (2) living beings without minds, and (3) minds that are somehow associated with animate bodies, and from them to (4) spiritual beings—minds without bodies.

Étienne Gilson summarizes the argument by saying that "the general plan of creation would display a manifest gap, if there were no angels." An orderly arrangement of the created universe involves "a hierarchy of created perfections" from the most perfect to the least perfect of creatures, i.e., from creatures that have the highest grade of being to creatures having the lowest. To this it must be added that all creatures share in the creaturely imperfection that consists in their dependence on God for their existence.

It is not surprising to find a reiteration of this reasoning by Dante who, in his *Convivio*, declared that, in an orderly universe, "the ascent and descent is by almost continuous steps, from the lowest form to the highest and from the highest to the lowest."

Dante then went on to say that "between the angelic nature . . .
and the human soul there is no intermediate step" as is also the
case "between the human soul and the most perfect soul of the
brute animals."

The same line of reasoning can be found in the work of a
seventeenth-century English empirical philosopher, John Locke.
In Book III, Chapter VI, Section 12 of his *Essay Concerning Human Understanding*, Locke observed that

in all the visible corporeal world we see no chasms or gaps. . . . Down
from us the descent is by easy steps. . . . There are some brutes that
seem to have as much reason and knowledge as some that are called
men; and the animal and vegetable kingdoms are so nearly joined that,
if you will take the lowest of one and the highest of the other, there
will scarce be perceived any great difference between them; and so on
until we come to the lowest and most unorganical parts of matter, we
shall find that the several species are linked together, and differ but in
almost insensible degrees.

In the light of this observation, Locke then continued as follows:

When we consider the infinite power and wisdom of the Maker, we
have reason to think that it is suitable to the magnificent harmony of
the universe, and the great design and infinite goodness of the architect,
that the species of creature should also, by gentle degrees, ascend upwards from us towards his infinite perfection, as we see them gradually
descend from us downwards.

Locke repeated this argument in Book IV, Chapter XVI, Section 12 of his *Essay*, but there he pointed out that, since the
reasoning rests on the principle of analogy, the conclusion it
reaches concerning the existence of angels is at best only probable, not certain. On this point, he differed from his philosophical contemporary and opponent, Gottfried Wilhelm Leibnitz, who
employed similar reasoning but regarded it as establishing the
conclusion with certitude.

In the same century, Sir Thomas Browne, in his *Religio Med-
ici*, expressed wonder that "so many learned heads should so far

forget their metaphysics, and destroy the ladder and scale of creatures, as to question the existence of spirits." This line of thought generally prevailed in the following century, too, and not exclusively in philosophical circles, though undoubtedly under the influence of John Locke.

The essayist Joseph Addison wrote, in one of his occasional papers, that

if the notion of a gradual rise in beings from the meanest to the most high be not a vain imagination, it is not improbable that an angel looks down upon a man, as a man doth upon a creature which approaches the nearest to the rational nature.

The poet Alexander Pope, in his *Essay on Man*, exclaimed:

> Vast chain of being! which from God began,
> Natures aethereal, human, angel, man,
> Beast, bird, fish, insect, what no eye can see,
> No glass can reach.

And a great American statesman, John Adams, echoed Pope, maintaining that "Nature, which has established a chain of being and a universal order in the universe, descending from angels to microscopic animalcules, has ordained that no two objects shall be perfectly alike and no two creatures perfectly equal."

(3) *The Great Chain of Being*

The theory of a great chain of being can be regarded either as a philosophical doctrine concerning the layout of Nature or as a theological doctrine concerning the design of a universe created by God.

Regarded in the second of these two ways, it provides the context for the theological explanation of why God created angels. Had God not done so, there would have been missing links in the chain—possibilities not realized.

Two assumptions seem to be involved in the explanation. One is that angels are genuinely possible beings that God could not omit without allowing gaps to occur in the great chain of being. We will consider the philosophical arguments for and against this assumption in Chapter 7 to follow.

The other assumption is that God either always acts for the best, or at least that the Divine will always chooses the better of two alternatives. The consequences of formulating this assumption in these two different ways will be examined in Section 4 of this chapter.

In his William James lectures at Harvard University in 1933, Professor Arthur O. Lovejoy explored the historical development of the idea of a great chain of being. His book based on the lectures richly deserves the high esteem in which it has been held as an extraordinarily comprehensive study in the history of ideas. Uncovering the origin of the idea in the writings of Plato and Aristotle and in the neo-Platonic philosophers of the Hellenistic period, surveying its development in the Middle Ages, and reporting in detail its recrudescence in the seventeenth and eighteenth centuries, Lovejoy's historical scholarship is almost flawless, but his account of the idea is marred by two serious mistakes in analysis that I hope to correct in what follows.

According to Lovejoy, the theory of a great chain of being rests on a pair of complementary principles. One of these he calls "the principle of plenitude."

For those unacquainted with the word "plenitude," let me say that, in Lovejoy's use of the term, it signifies a fullness, a completeness, an abundance to which nothing can be added. It envisions a perfect or complete universe as one in which all possibilities are realized.

Lovejoy attributes the earliest formulation of this principle to Plato and calls attention to the fact that Aristotle rejected it, because the realm of possibilities may include incompatible opposites. Hence the realization of all possibilities would have to consist in the realization of all that are *compossible* (i.e., simultaneously compatible), or perhaps it involves the successive realization of incompatible possibilities.

Lovejoy attributes the other of the two fundamental principles to Aristotle and calls it "the principle of continuity." In thus conceiving and naming it, he makes a mistake that consists in an erroneous interpretation of Aristotle and also one that makes the principle of continuity inapplicable to the great chain of being in which angels are indispensable links.

This principle should have been described, at least so far as Aristotle and angels are concerned, as a principle that calls for an orderly array or arrangement of all the possibilities to be realized in compliance with the principle of plentitude. An orderly arrangement can take two forms, both of which Aristotle discussed, but only one of which applies to angels as links in the great chain of being.

In one form, an orderly arrangement embodies what Lovejoy calls the principle of continuity. He uses the word "continuity" in a sense that does not conform to the strict mathematical usage that has been developed in the theory of continuum. I will adopt Lovejoy's much looser sense of the term. What he means by a continuous series or sequence is one in which each member differs only in degree from its nearest neighbors; and also one in which one or more others can always be introduced between any two members of the series.

The sequence of fractions between zero and one is continuous in Lovejoy's sense of the term, but not in the strict mathematical sense of it. Each fraction in the sequence is less than another on one side of it and more than another on the other side of it; and between any two given fractions, there are an indefinite number of intermediates.

In his biological works, Aristotle viewed nature as an orderly arrangement that has something like such continuity. There is a famous passage in his *History of Animals*, one that Lovejoy quotes, in which Aristotle said that "Nature proceeds from things lifeless to animal life in such a way that it is impossible to determine the exact line of demarcation, nor on which side thereof an intermediate form should lie." He then went on to say that "there is observed in plants a continuous scale of ascent toward the animal."

The other form of an orderly arrangement embodies the principle of hierarchy. It calls for the ordering of things in a scale of perfections in which each rank differs in kind, not degree, from the one below and the one above. A simple mathematical example is the sequence of integers or whole numbers, or the sequence of regular polygons in plane geometry.

In such sequences, there are no gaps or breaks. But unlike the sequence of fractions, a hierarchical sequence does not permit the presence of intermediates between any two proximate members of the series. There can be no intermediate whole number between 1 and 2 or between 3 and 4; no intermediate polygon between a triangle and a square or between a square and a pentagon.

If the absence of unfilled gaps justifies Lovejoy's calling a sequence continuous, then the sequence of whole numbers or of regular polygons can be regarded as continuous. But if, in his meaning of "continuous," a sequence should be called "continuous" *only* if there are always intermediates between any two of its members, then only the sequence of fractions is "continuous" and the sequence of whole numbers or regular polygons is not.

In his philosophical works, Aristotle viewed nature as an orderly arrangement that is a scale of beings differing in kind, not in degree. The order of kinds or species, conceived as involving essential differences, not merely difference in degree, is in Aristotle's view a hierarchical arrangement. Both in his *Metaphysics* and in his treatise *On the Soul*, he repeatedly compared the order of kinds or species to the sequence of whole numbers or the sequence of regular polygons.

Professor Lovejoy, unfortunately, failed to see that the orderly arrangement constituting a great chain of being can take the form of a hierarchical series of species or kinds as well as the form of a continuous series in which there are only differences in degree.

Perceiving that a hierarchical order of kinds or species cannot be continuous in the same sense that the sequence of fractions is continuous, Lovejoy failed to recognize that a hierarchical, like a continuous, array may nevertheless have no missing links. If he had recognized this point, he would have seen that the principle of continuity is not needed to complement the principle of plenitude. The principle of hierarchy serves that purpose equally well.

In addition, if Lovejoy had remembered that in the realm of spiritual creatures, each angel is a distinct species and differs essentially from every other angel in kind, he would have been led inexorably to the conclusion that the orderly arrangement of a universe that includes angels must consist in a hierarchical ladder of beings essentially distinct in kind, not a continuous series constituted only by differences in degree.

It may be helpful to consider nonmathematical examples of a hierarchical arrangement as contrasted with a continuous series involving only differences in degree.

The percentage ranking of baseball pitchers and hitters very roughly exemplifies a sequence of differences in degree. Between any two degrees of excellence in the sport, an intermediate is likely to occur, having a higher rating than one and a lower rating than the other.

In contrast, a military organization exemplifies a hierarchy. It is constituted by various grades of noncommissioned officers and various ranks of commissioned officers. Between a private first class and a corporal, between a second lieutenant and a first lieutenant, between a colonel and a one-star general, and so on, there are no intermediate ranks. The whole scale of ranks can be completely filled, leaving no intermediates between any two ranks.

The difference between a hierarchical and a continuous ascent or descent can also be expressed as follows. It is like the difference between going up or down a ladder and going up or down a rope or slide.

When St. Thomas Aquinas expounds the Dionysian theory of the hierarchy of angels, he certainly has the hierarchical type of orderly arrangement in mind. This is confirmed by the arguments he advances in another place, to the effect that angels differ from one another as essentially distinct species differ, not accidentally or in degree as individual members of a single species do.

Contrary to what John Adams thought, all human beings are specifically equal as members of the human species. They are also unequal as individuals, differing in degree from one another in a wide variety of respects. But because no two angels are individually different members of the same species, no two angels are specifically equal.

In Chapter 8, I will have more to say about this and its philosophical significance for our understanding of the theory of species in the realm of corporeal things. Here I wish only to point out that it would be odd, to say the least, if, in the realm of corporeal things, the orderly arrangement were governed solely by the principle of continuity, while in the realm of spiritual creatures, it was governed by the principle of hierarchy.

That would be like a military organization in which the noncommissioned personnel differed from one another only in a continuous series of degrees, while the commissioned officers differed from one another in a hierarchical series of ranks. A well-planned military organization would certainly not be like that, nor would a well-designed universe created by a deity who always acted to produce the best result, or at least a better rather than worse one.

(4) *The Best of All Possible Worlds*

The second mistake in Lovejoy's treatment of the theory of a great chain of being lies in his misunderstanding of the theological aspects of the theory. The error consists in thinking that the universe that God created would be constituted by a plenitude of beings, with no possibilities unrealized, *only* if God were under the necessity or compulsion to create the best of all possible worlds.

According to this view of the matter, God is deprived of freedom of choice. As Lovejoy sees it, a theologian like Thomas Aquinas is impaled on the horns of the following dilemma: *either*

(a) he must abandon his belief that God has freedom of choice *or* (b) he cannot cogently argue that angels must exist. If they did not exist, the universe that God created would be imperfect. The possibility of spiritual beings would be unrealized and so it would be lacking what a more perfect universe would contain.

To say, on the one hand, that God in creating is free to choose a less than perfect universe, and to say, on the other hand, that God must have created angels because the universe he created would have been less than perfect without them, is to contradict oneself. Lovejoy is certainly right on that score, but wrong in thinking that Aquinas' treatment of the matter exhibits this contradiction.

He is wrong for a number of reasons, the first of which is that, as a theologian, Aquinas does not attempt to prove by reasoning that angels exist. His affirmation of their existence expresses a scripturally based article of religious faith.

As I pointed out earlier in this chapter, neither a theological nor a philosophical argument can be constructed to prove the existence of angels. All that philosophical reasoning can do in the service of the dogmatic theologian concerned with the question of angelic existence is to help him explain why he believes what, in fact, he does believe. The explanation proceeds by the following steps.

Step 1. We know by reason and beyond a reasonable doubt, as I have argued elsewhere, that God, an infinite and purely spiritual being, exists. Here the theologian relies upon the philosopher for the reasoning involved, reasoning that has some measure of probative force but falls short of certitude. I have employed such reasoning in a book entitled *How to Think About God.*

Step 2. We believe by religious faith, if we believe at all, that the God affirmed to exist by the philosopher is infinitely powerful, wise, and good—that his omnipotence enables him to do everything that is possible, and that his wisdom and goodness incline him to order things for the best. Here the theologian goes beyond anything that the philosopher can say if the philosopher strictly limits himself to what his reason is able to establish.

Step 3. We believe, again by religious faith, that the infinite perfection of the Divine being includes perfect freedom—freedom to create or not to create; and, freely choosing to create, freedom to create one or another among all the universes that are possible, of which the present universe is only one.

In the section of the *Summa Theologica* that is concerned with the power of God (Question 25, Articles 5 and 6), Aquinas unequivocally asserts that God could have created other universes than the one that now exists and that he could have created a better universe than the present.

If the theologian takes this third step, he would appear to fail in his effort to explain why God, in creating this universe, included angels among the creatures that he brought into being. That may be why Lovejoy supposes that the theologian must avoid taking it.

If he is going to prove that God created angels as links in the great chain of being, he must think of God as being unfree—as being under the necessity of creating the best of all possible worlds.

However, there is a fourth step in the theologian's thinking, one that Lovejoy ignores. It consists in his religious belief that angels or spiritual creatures in fact exist in this particular universe that God created. That is for the theologian a scripturally based article of faith, not something to be proved by rational argument.

Given *Step 4,* (the belief that angels do in fact exist), the theologian need only answer the question: *Why, then, did God create angels, if he was under no necessity to do so?* Having freedom of choice, according to Step 3, God does not have to create the best of all possible worlds—a world constituted by a great chain of being that includes a hierarchy of spiritual creatures.

Step 5, the last step in this line of thought, consists in the theologian's answer to the question raised in Step 4. Among the possible universes God might have created, one that includes angels is better than one in which they are lacking.

God was free to create a universe less perfect than the present one that He did in fact create. He was also free to create a universe better than the present one. Better or worse possibilities aside, the actual universe that God did create has a certain measure of perfection because it includes both spiritual and corporeal creatures.

That explains why God, in creating this universe, did in fact create angels. It does not prove that angels must exist in any universe created by God because God must create the best of all possible worlds.

It was the eighteenth-century German philosopher Liebnitz who argued in that way, not the mediaeval theologian Aquinas. An argument of this sort would also have been congenial to an ancient philosopher such as Plotinus or to a modern philosopher such as Spinoza, both of whom denied God freedom of choice and conceived him as always acting under a necessity imposed on him by his own nature.

However, Plotinus was not a Christian philosopher, and Spinoza was a Jew whose philosophical doctrine brought down upon his head the anathema of the Jewish community that charged him with heresy. For Leibnitz, who was a Christian philosopher, an argument that involves the notion that God is under a necessity to create the best of all possible worlds must be embarrassing.

The contradiction in it that Lovejoy wrongly attributes to Aquinas does impale Leibnitz on the horns of an uncomfortable dilemma. It does so because he tried to establish rationally that a great chain of being including angels *must exist*. If the reason is that God *must create the best of all possible worlds*, then the reason for thinking that angels *must exist* is also the reason for thinking that God *cannot be free*.

In sharp contrast, Aquinas does not think that angels *must exist*. He simply believes that they *do exist* and he can explain that belief and make it reasonable without denying freedom to God.

5

Theological Speculation About Angels

(1) *The Range and Order of Questions*

WE HAVE now examined the theologian's answer to the question about the reality of angels as spiritual creatures. The questions that remain for him to consider concern the attributes and actions of angels.

Just as the anthropologist is concerned with investigating the attributes of human nature and the characteristic activities of the human race, so the angelologist is concerned with the attributes of the angelic nature and the kind of activity that angels typically perform.

Anthropology—the study of man—is a double-barrelled discipline. It is in part a branch of scientific inquiry, conducted by empirical methods of observation. It is also in part a branch of philosophical thought, consisting in reflective analysis. Their methods being so different, the scientific and the philosophical study of man do not attempt to answer the same questions. Each deals with questions that are appropriate to its type of inquiry— questions it is able to answer by the method it employs.

Angelology—the study of angels—also divides into two distinct types of inquiry, one philosophical, the other theological. The latter deals with those questions that are generated by scripturally based articles of faith; the former with those questions that can be asked about angels without any reference to religious beliefs. In this chapter, we will consider only the theological

[68]

questions about the nature and actions of angels, reserving philosophical questions for Chapter 8.

Not only are the questions different for the theologian and the philosopher; so also is the order in which the questions should be taken up.

The philosopher finds it is appropriate to begin with questions about the nature and attributes of angels and then to turn to questions about how they act and what they do.

The proper order for the theologian, it seems to me, should be the reverse. Questions that arise from the consideration of what is said in Sacred Scriptures about the mission of angels should come first. Euclidating what angels do helps to throw light on what angels are.

I am aware that, to proceed in this way, is to depart from the order followed by Thomas Aquinas in the *Summa Theologica*. Even though he was writing a strictly theological treatise, Aquinas' interest in angels was largely philosophical. From the philosopher's point of view, the nature and attributes of a certain kind of being should be considered before one undertakes to discuss its operations or functions.

There may be another justification for the order that Aquinas follows. As we saw in Chapter 4, the *raison d'être* for angels in the Divine plan is not the mission they perform on earth. It is the role that the heavenly host plays in the perfection of the created universe.

The action of angels on earth and in relation to human beings is, in fact, performed only by *some* angels, not by *all*, not even by *most*. In the main, the life of angels—of *all* angels, even those who carry messages to mankind or have earthly missions to perform—consists in what they do in heaven, not what they do on earth.

Nevertheless, for the purpose of this exposition of theological thought about angels, I am going to deal first with questions about the mission of angels on earth, and second with questions about the life of angels in heaven.

With regard to each question to be faced, I am going to state briefly the theologian's answer. When I refer to "the theologian," the reference is always to Thomas Aquinas. In doing so, I am following his own custom of using such phrases as "the philosopher," "the commentator," and "the rabbi," to refer, respectively, to Aristotle, to Averroës, the Arabic disciple of Aristotle, and to the great Jewish teacher, Moses Maimonides.

When other theologians differ from Aquinas on some point of importance, I will call attention to this fact.

(2) *The Mission of Angels on Earth*

With regard to the mission of angels, the theologian raises four questions.

1. Are any angels sent forth on missions?
2. Are all angels sent forth?
3. Do those who are sent forth remain in God's presence?
4. From what angelic orders are they sent forth?

In answering the first question, the theologian finds his controlling text in *Exodus* 23:20—"Behold, I will send my angels to go before thee."

A minister, the theologian tells us, "is an instrument with intelligence." The ministry performed by angels at God's behest is instrumental in the Divine government of the corporeal world, especially in manifesting God's providence with respect to the human race.

Angels not only carry messages from God to man. They also influence human action in other ways, and they act directly on the physical environment that is the stage on which human action takes place.

It would appear from a question asked by St. Paul in his *Epistle to the Hebrews* (1:14)—"Are not all the ministering spirits sent forth?"—that the answer to the second question should turn out to be affirmative. But here the theologian cites the approval given by St. Gregory the Great to a statement by Dionysius declaring "the higher ranks of angels perform no exterior service."

The exterior service referred to is the angelic ministry that is performed on earth with respect to human beings and their environment. Such angelic activity falls mainly, but not exclusively, to the two lowest orders of angels. "Those who announce the highest things," the theologian writes, "are called archangels," and he goes on to point out that it is "the archangel Gabriel who was sent to the Virgin Mary" to announce the blessed event. Below archangels, the lowest order, simply called angels, perform lesser ministries.

Considering the nine orders in the three-tiered hierarchy of the heavenly host, the theologian divides them into the upper four and the lower five, and says that the earthly ministry of the celestial spirits is carried out only by the lower five. The upper four, he maintains, never leave heaven on errands or missions in the execution of the Divine will.

Nevertheless, while answering the fourth question in this way, the theologian, in response to the third question, also declares that since all members of the heavenly host receive, through God's grace, the power to see the Divine essence directly, all—not just the upper ranks—live constantly in the presence of God. Here he relies on the authority of St. Gregory who said that even those angels who are sent by God on external ministries for our salvation "always stand in the Divine presence and see the face of the Father."

Sacred Scripture contains many passages in which angels are described in one or another bodily form, sometimes human, sometimes not. Some have maintained, the theologian acknowledges, that "angels never assume bodies, and that all the angelic appearances of which we read in the Scriptures were prophetic visions; that is, they took place in the imagination of the persons" who report these angelic visitations. The theologian rejects this view as being contrary to the sense of Scriptures.

"What is seen only in someone's imagination," he argues,

is a purely private experience; it is not a thing that anyone else can see at the same time. But the Scriptures speak of angels appearing visibly to everyone who happened to be present at a given place; those seen by

Abraham, for example, were also seen by his servants, and those seen by Lot were also seen by the people of Sodom.

The theologian is quick to point out that since angels are purely spiritual beings, totally incorporeal and without being burdened by a body to which they are united, the bodies in which angels appear to men must be merely "assumed bodies"—bodies that they take on "not for their own sake, but for ours," in order to perform their ministry to us.

A twentieth-century disciple of Aquinas, Father Walter Farrell, O.P., elucidates the point by observing that an angel's assuming a body is like a man's hiring a dress suit for a particular occasion. "As to where they got the bodies," he adds, "any answer is no more than a guess."

However, about one aspect of this matter the theologian can give an answer that is much less conjectural. The bodies that angels assume for their earthly ministry are not really living bodies. They only appear to be so. [Strictly speaking, they are like masks, which are not real visages but deceptive counterfeits of faces.] These assumed bodies cannot perform any of the vital functions that properly belong to living organisms.

So far we have considered the ministry of angels in general—as messengers from God to man and as instruments in the execution of Divine providence. There is another service that angels perform in relation to human life and in the furtherance of human salvation. That consists in their role as guardian angels.

To each of the following questions, the theologian gives an affirmative answer.

1. Are there guardian angels?
2. Is a single guardian angel assigned to each individual human being?
3. Are the guardian angels drawn exclusively from the lowest rank of angels?
4. Does every human being have his own guardian angel?
5. Does the angelic guardianship of each human being begin at the moment of birth?

6. Do guardian angels always watch over the individuals they are assigned to guard, never for a moment forsaking their duty in this respect?

In answering these questions, the theologian relies mainly on the authority of St. Jerome's commentary on various passages in the Psalms, as, for example, the statement by the Psalmist that "He has given His angels charge over you to guard you in all your ways." In the opinion of Father Farrell, the assignment of angels to the guardianship of human beings is "a fact completely certain from abundant places in Holy Scripture."

Not all theologians agree that the role of guardian angels is so clearly supported by Scripture. "Whether each of the faithful has a particular angel assigned him for his defence," John Calvin writes, "I cannot venture certainly to affirm." Citing the declaration by Christ that "the angels of children always behold the face of the Father," Calvin concedes that this may suggest that "certain angels are charged with their safety." Nevertheless, he doubts that "this justifies the conclusion that every one of them has a particular guardian angel." He prefers to think that "not one angel only has the care of every one of us, but that all the angels together with one consent watch over our salvation."

The disputed question concerning guardian angels, and especially the difference of opinion concerning whether each human being has his own guardian angel, involves another much disputed question about the number of angels.

If there is a single guardian angel for each human being, and if the guardian angels are drawn exclusively from the lowest rank in the nine orders of angels, it would appear to follow that, for these reasons alone, the population of heaven must exceed the human population on earth. The theologian's estimate of the number is greater than that; for he asserts that the number of spiritual beings vastly surpasses the number of material things.

The scriptural warrant for this assertion comes from the *Book of Daniel* (7:10), where it is said that "thousands upon thousands ministered to Him, and ten thousand times a hundred thousand

stood before Him." Whatever the exact number is, it was fixed
at the instant of creation. The human population changes in the
course of time, but the multitude of the heavenly host neither
waxes nor wanes through all eternity.

Here once again John Calvin does not see eye to eye with
Thomas Aquinas. "Let those who venture to determine the
number of angels," he cautions, "examine on what foundation
their opinions rest." Calvin concedes that Sacred Scripture contains statements by Christ concerning many myriads of angels,
and by the servant of Elisha who reported seeing many chariots
of angels. But he thinks that the question of the exact number
of angels cannot be answered by us. It belongs "to that class of
mysteries, the full revelation of which is deferred to the last day."

Two matters remain with respect to the earthly mission of
angels. One is concerned with how angels act upon material
things, especially those that surround human beings and affect
their lives and actions. The other is concerned with how angels
act on human individuals.

The theologian holds the view that the world of material things
is subject to control by angels. Even though they are minds
without bodies, they have the power to effect bodily changes,
especially change of place. "Just as the lower angels . . . are
controlled by the higher ones," Aquinas writes, "so material
things are controlled by angels. This is the position not only of
the doctors of the church, but also of all the philosophers who
postulate the existence of nonmaterial beings."

Here Aquinas has especially in mind the Aristotelian theory
of the spiritual beings who move the celestial spheres, though he
also refers to the views held by Plato and by the Arabic philosopher Avicenna.

The power of the angels over material things is, of course,
subject in all respects to the power of God. It is God's will, not
the will of angels, to which material things are obedient. And
while angels can cause bodily alterations and the motion of bodies from one place to another, they cannot produce miracles.
Only God can do that.

Our difficulty in understanding the views of the theologian concerning the action of angels on corporeal things can be explained, Father Farrell writes,

by our insistence on carrying over the imagery of human activity into the world of angels. We argue that because a man cannot throw a ball without hands, of course an angel is just as helpless. The fact is that a body limits and contracts the activity of a spiritual substance rather than aids it.

We cannot move other bodies except through our own body. The angel, not suffering this limitation, can move bodies without resorting to corporeal instrumentalities, but that fact makes "it impossible for us to draw imaginative pictures of the process."

We come finally to questions about how angels act upon human beings. According to the theologian, the human intellect can be enlightened by angels in a manner somewhat analogous to the way in which one human being teaches another. Just as no human teacher can pour ideas or knowledge into the mind of a learner, neither can angels instruct men by putting ideas or insights into their minds.

No human being can act directly on the intellect of another, but only indirectly by affecting the latter's sense experience and imagination. Teaching is done through words, gestures, diagrams, and pictures—all belonging to the realm of sense experience and imagination. Angels teach men in similar fashion. Having power over bodies, they influence the operation of the human intellect by affecting the bodily organs of sense and imagination.

Likewise, angels cannot directly determine acts of the human will. The inviolability of its freedom exempts it from such determination either by angels or by men. But just as one human being can influence the will of another by efforts at persuasion, or by motivating it in one or another way through arousing emotions, so angels have even greater power to influence the will of individuals in these indirect ways.

As Father Farrell points out, this

demands nothing extraordinary on the part of the angels; if they can move material things locally, they can stimulate our senses and imagination. Unlike the intellect and the will, our senses and our imagination can be got at from the outside.

(3) *A Necessary Digression*

Readers who are unaccustomed to following the process of theological thought and who are prone to suspect that it is speculation of the wildest sort may be puzzled by the character of the questions about angels to which the theologian addresses himself.

The puzzlement of such readers may be magnified by the fact that many of these questions do not seem to be forced upon the theologian by scriptural passages calling for theological explanation. If Sacred Scripture does not require such questions to be posed, why did the theologian raise them? Just in order to engage in speculation for its own sake? If so, the theological enterprise is hardly a respectable one and does not deserve serious intellectual consideration.

If some readers have formed this erroneous impression, I think it can and should be corrected. Hence this digression in order to show that theological speculation has, in its own way, a rigor comparable to that of mathematical reasoning. Far from being wild and uncontrolled, it is led inexorably from its initial premises to certain conclusions. In the framework of dogmatic theology, these premises are furnished by scripturally based beliefs.

In the theological speculation about angels that we have just reviewed, there are two initial premises, both scripturally based. One is the belief that angels are purely spiritual creatures. The other is the belief that, while all angels in their heavenly life engage in the contemplation of God, some in their earthly visitations are instruments of Divine providence in the guidance of human affairs.

From these two premises, it follows, first, that whether or not they perform a ministry on earth, all angels are always in the presence of God. It follows, second, that the bodies angels are described in Sacred Scriptures as having must be assumed bodies—not real bodies, but counterfeits thereof. It follows, third, that angels must be able to act directly on bodies in the physical environment of man and on the human body as well, in order to act indirectly on the intellects and wills of human beings.

Were these things not so, angels could not carry out the missions that they are reported in Sacred Scriptures as performing; nor would they have any life at all when they are not engaged in the exterior service that is their ministry on earth.

Two things do not follow from the initial premises as stated, and it would seem to be the case that Sacred Scripture does not require the theologian to consider them.

One is whether the number of angels is larger or smaller than the number of material things. The other is whether each individual human being has his very own guardian angel. As we have seen, these are matters of dispute among theologians. It is quite appropriate that that should be the case, for these two points in angelology are like undecidable propositions in an otherwise rigorous mathematical system.

(4) *The Life of Angels in Heaven*

Sacred Scripture is for the most part silent with regard to the life of the angels in heaven. There are a few exceptions; as, for example, the passage in the prophet Zacharias (1:12), in which the angel of the Lord addresses God, saying "O Lord of Hosts, how long wilt thou not have mercy on Jerusalem?" This text supports the theologian's affirmative answer to the question whether angels speak to God. To most other questions about the angels in heaven, in relation to God and to each other, the theologian appears to proceed without such support.

That Sacred Scriptures do not touch on these matters is not surprising. The Divine revelation that they contain is intended for the enlightenment of mankind, not the angelic host, and that enlightenment is intended to provide mankind with knowledge about God that he cannot attain through the exercise of his natural faculties, and with an understanding of his place and destiny in the Divine design that he cannot arrive at by his own wits.

In the latter connection, the precepts of Divine law are revealed to him as well as the gifts of God's grace, the one as a guide, the other as a help, in man's striving for salvation. It is in this connection, that the revelation concerning the ministry of angels on earth becomes relevant, for that plays a role in God's scheme of salvation for man. But how angels in heaven act in relation to God and to each other and how their lives are blessed by God's gifts have little or no bearing on the course of human life in the pursuit of its ultimate end.

The absence of scriptural references to such matters would appear to preclude the dogmatic theologian from dealing with them, leaving them for consideration by the philosopher who is entitled to speculate about them without any guidance from Divine revelation.

How far, then, can the theologian go in dealing with such matters? And what is his warrant for going further than he is required to in his effort to understand what is revealed about angels?

The answer is as follows. As we have seen in the preceding pages, Sacred Scripture controls what the dogmatic theologian has to say about the mission of angels on earth. With regard to the life of angels in heaven, the theologian is warranted in drawing whatever conclusions logically follow from other matters that are determined by the framework of his religious beliefs. This far he can go, but no further.

We have seen that the theologian thinks that angels are creatures superior to men but that, as creatures, they are inferior to God. Hence they can do what men cannot do, but cannot do what God can do. So, too, their life involves change but not growth, whereas human life involves growth and decline as well as change, and there is neither change nor growth in the life of God.

Within this framework, the theologian gives a negative answer to the question whether angels have eternal life. Nothing created can be eternal—without beginning or end and without any trace of mutability. Being created, the angels came into existence at the very beginning of things when God created both heaven and earth. Being immaterial, they cannot cease to be, as living organisms cease to be when death and disintegration befalls them. They have immortal life as, according to the theologian, the human soul also has immortal life, continuing to subsist after its separation from its mortal body.

To name the middle ground between (a) *time*, in which all corporeal creatures have their mutable existence, and (b) *eternity*, in which God exists immutably without beginning or end, the theologian calls it (c) *aeviternity*. "Aeviternity," he writes, "differs from time and eternity as the mean between them both." He goes on to explain this as follows.

Eternity is the measure of permanent being; insofar as anything recedes from permanence of being it recedes from eternity. Now some things recede from permanence of being, so that their being is subject to change, or consists in change, and these things are measured by time. . . . But others recede less from permanence of being, because their being neither consists in change, nor is subject to change; nevertheless they have change annexed to them. . . . This applies to the angels, who have an unchangeable being together with changeableness as regards choice, which pertains to their nature; moreover, they have changeableness of intelligence, of affections, and of places, in their own degree. Therefore, these are measured by aeviternity, which is a mean between eternity and time.

God alone exists from all eternity and completely transcends time and change. The angels are above time as a measure of change and motion in the physical universe. Precisely because it is intrinsically mutable, the physical universe is neither eternal nor aeviternal, even were it without beginning and end.

Since Sacred Scripture reveals that both heaven and earth did have a beginning, neither corporeal nor spiritual creatures are eternal; but the different ways in which they are subject to change differentiates the time in which corporeal things exist from the aeviternity of the angels. On this point, two great theologians appear to differ.

Where Aquinas attributes to the angels an aeviternal life that is neither temporal nor eternal, but a middle ground between them, Bonaventure holds that they have an aeviternal existence so far as the permanence or imperishability of their being is concerned, but that their existence also has a temporal aspect. It continually needs to be sustained and preserved by God and it is also subject to certain types of change, different from the change that corporeal things undergo.

Superior to human beings who have minds conjoined with bodies, the angels—minds without bodies—know without any dependence on sense-experience or imagination and have wills with freedom of choice but without being subject to the influence of bodily passions. Being mere creatures and so infinitely remote from the supreme being and perfection of their creator, the acts of knowledge and love of which angels are capable have definite limitations.

By the knowing that is inherent in their created natures, they cannot know the future; only God's omniscience extends to that. By such natural knowledge, they cannot know God as God knows himself, nor can they know the mysterious working of Divine grace.

Just as man's natural knowledge is transcended by the supernatural knowledge that is a gift of God, so too the angels, as recipients of Divine grace, enjoy the vision of God that is the blessedness and glory of life in heaven.

By the knowledge with which their natures are endowed at creation, each angel knows himself reflexively, knows other angels, and knows the corporeal things of this world. Being unequal in their created natures, the superior angels know all these things to a higher degree and to a greater extent than inferior angels do.

Angels of different rank can communicate with one another, the higher angels enlightening the lower, while the lower can only manifest their state of mind to the higher. That angels do speak to one another, but not with voice, word, or gesture as in human communication, is supported by the scriptural passage in which the Apostle Paul says "I speak with the tongues of men and of angels."

The enlightenment that superior angels can confer upon inferior angels when they speak to them is limited to knowledge of the created universe; it does not extend to knowledge of God. Only God can confer such enlightenment on creatures, whether angels or human beings. Though one angel can enlighten another, it cannot determine the act of another's will. Only God can do that.

When angels speak to God, they merely manifest their state of mind to their creator, just as inferior angels only manifest their state of mind to superior angels. The same is true of the speech of men to angels, as this is recorded in Sacred Scripture. Men cannot teach or enlighten angels in any way, but they can make their own state of mind known to angels by manifesting it to them.

Just as the angelic nature is endowed with knowledge at its creation, so also is it endowed with love, a love that accords with the two precepts of charity that Christ enjoined mankind to observe. Each angel loves God before self and loves fellow angels in a measure equal to self-love.

The love that is connatural to angels is as imperfect as the knowledge that is connnatural to them—connatural in the sense of being something with which their natures are endowed when created. It needs to be elevated or perfected by the supernatural gifts of God's grace. Beatitude, which consists in such supernatural knowledge and love of God, is enjoyed only by angels who are elevated to glory by God's grace.

An act of free choice on their part separates the angels in heaven and in a state of grace from the angels that fell from heaven into the kingdom of darkness where they are deprived of the Divine light that enables the blessed angels to see God. We will consider hell's angels and the mystery of their sinful choice in the following chapter.

There we will deal with matters that belong exclusively to dogmatic theology and are entirely beyond the reach of philosophical speculation. That is not the case with respect to many of the points of theological doctrine that have been briefly summarized in this chapter. While they can be treated by the dogmatic theologian within the framework of his religious beliefs, they are also open to philosophical speculation without any reference to religious dogmas or doctrines.

Much that has been merely touched on here will be more fully explored, especially with an eye to its significance for human life, in the chapters of Part Three that deal with angels as objects of philosophical thought.

6

Hell's Angels

(1) *From Heaven to Hell*

AT THE MOMENT of their creation, all of God's angels are
in heaven. A moment later, if one can speak of anything like
temporal succession in aeviternity, some are no longer there. They
have committed the first—the original—sin in defiance of God.
They have dropped out of heaven and fallen into hell.

If heaven—or Paradise as it is sometimes called—is not a
physical place, then neither is hell. Both are states of spiritual
being, the one a realm of light in the presence of God, the other
a realm of darkness devoid of that light and of that presence.

All the words we use to talk about heaven and hell must be
understood in purely spiritual terms, appropriate to their being
states of mind in purely spiritual beings. Such words as "light,"
"darkness," and "presence" must be shorn of their physical
connotations.

The light that shines on the blessed angels is the supernatural
knowledge of God's essence that is a gift of God's grace. The
darkness into which the damned are thrown is the deprivation
of such knowledge. To know God with God's help as God knows
himself is to be in God's presence.

From the early days of Christianity, throughout the Middle
Ages, and right down to our time, not only hell-fire and brim-
stone preachers, but also learned theologians have evaded or
transgressed the strictures against physical interpretations that,
in my judgment, must be obeyed. The joys of the blessed in

heaven and the pains of the damned in hell have been described as if they were sensible and fleshly, not just intellectual and spiritual. If the trappings of the senses and the flesh once were or still are ingredients in orthodox religious beliefs concerning heaven and hell, the beliefs in question, I am compelled to say, cannot be defended by reason. They stand in violation of it.*

Dante's *Inferno* and the opening books of Milton's *Paradise Lost* employ exceptionally vivid physical imagery to describe the torments of hell. That is required for the purposes of poetry. But the purposes of poetry and of theology are as different as the requirements of the imagination and of the intellect. What is appropriate in the one is out of place in the other.

The division of the angels into those that remain in the presence of God and those that turn away from God—in both cases, by their own free choice—raises problems of the utmost difficulty for the dogmatic theologian. Before we explore those problems and consider the solutions that have been proposed, it is necessary, first, to survey the dogmas and the doctrines that have been developed in this area of angelology.

The Old and New Testaments are replete with references to the fallen angels, spoken of as devils and demons, and to their leader who goes by the name of Satan or Lucifer. The Hebrew word from which "Satan" is derived literally means the adversary or enemy. The Latin roots of "Lucifer" give that name the connotation of light-bearing.

Both names and their meanings are appropriate to the character of the highest of all the angels God created, superior to all other creatures. He is by his created nature most effulgent with the light of knowledge. He is also, by his own free choice, most opposed to God and to the ultimate good of mankind.

Up to this point, the theories about angels we have been examining have been shared, in most of their essentials, by dogmatic theologians in all three of the Western religions—Judaism,

---

*The doctrine of the resurrection of the body and the dogmas concerning certain resurrected bodies is rendered consistent with this point by the notion that such bodies are spiritual rather than physical.

Christianity, and Islam. That cannot be said about the dogmas and the doctrines concerning the sin of Satan and the fallen angels. Here we confront beliefs that are peculiar to Christianity and distinctive of it.

The sin of Satan and the role he plays in relation to Adam and Eve are inseparable from the belief in Jesus Christ as the incarnation in human form of the second person of the triune Godhead and as mankind's redeemer from sin. God became man and suffered on the cross to expiate the sin that barred mankind from salvation. The doctrine of original sin, and of its happy ending through mankind's redemption by Christ crucified and Christ risen, lies at the heart of Christianity as a religion, and is foreign to both Judaism and Islam.

In their appended essay on Satan, the editors of the Blackfriars edition of the *Summa Theologica* of Thomas Aquinas stress the centrality of Satan in both Catholic and Protestant Christianity. Satan, they write, "is part and parcel of the Christian religion . . . no Satan, no Christ; that is both a historical and a theological truth."

In that same essay, the writers provide us with a summary of the dogmas of Roman Catholic Christianity with regard to Satan, dogmas that have their basis in the New Testament.

At the Fourth Lateran Council, it was declared to be a matter of faith that "Satan and the other devils are by nature spirits," that "they were created by God, and so were originally good, but fell into sin of their own free will," and that "they are eternally damned."

To this, the Fourth Lateran Council added the further article of faith that "the first man, Adam, sinned at the devil's instigation"; and in consequence, according to the Council of Trent, "passed into the devil's powers, and with him the human race that was to descend from him."

The two great Protestant reformers expressed views that are not essentially dissimilar. Martin Luther's *Table Talk* is full of references to Satan and to the devils under his command. In one very telling passage, he writes as follows:

The acknowledgment of angels is needful in the church. Therefore godly preachers should teach them logically. First, they should show what angels are, namely, spiritual creatures without bodies. Secondly, what manner of spirits they are, namely, good spirits and not evil, and here evil spirits must be spoken of, not created evil by God, but made so by their rebellion against God, and their consequent fall; this hatred began in Paradise, and will continue and remain against Christ and his church to the world's end.

. . . The devil is also near and about us, incessantly tracking our steps, in order to deprive us of our lives, our saving health, and salvation. But the holy angels defend us from him, insomuch that he is not able to work up such mischief as willingly he would.

In his *Institutes of the Christian Religion,* John Calvin tells us that "since the devil was created by God . . . this wickedness which we attribute to his nature is not from creation, but from corruption. . . . Let us be content," he continues, "with this concise information concerning the nature of devils; that at their creation, they were originally angels of God, but by degenerating have ruined themselves, and become the instruments of perdition to others."

Nevertheless, Calvin adds, Satan "can do nothing against God's will and consent." Satan "attempts those things which he thinks most opposed to God," but "God holds him tied and bound with the bridle of his power," so that he can do "only those things which are divinely permitted."

In the *Summa Theologica* of Thomas Aquinas the discussion of these matters is more elaborate. It is full of subtleties. It is also more carefully and precisely conducted. Questions 62, 63, and 64 are, respectively, concerned with the raising of the angels to the state of grace and glory, with the sin of Satan and the other fallen angels, and with their consequent punishment. For our present purposes, let it suffice to state some of the points made.

According to Aquinas, the angels were not created in a state of bliss, which consists in being confirmed in goodness by the gift of God's grace; for if that were the case, no angel could have turned away from God. "The fall of some angels," he writes, "shows that the angelic nature was not created in that state."

Aquinas then explains that "to see the essence of God, which is the ultimate bliss of the rational creature, is beyond every created intellect's natural power. . . . Therefore, no angel could of his own will turn towards that bliss unless aided by grace." On the other hand, he also maintains that the blessed angels merited bliss by their first act of charity—that act by which their love of God manifested a willingness to receive God's grace. Once blessed, the good angels are confirmed in goodness. They cannot sin. Seeing God's essence, they cannot turn away.

Against this background, Aquinas then considered the angels who sinned. Because, like man, they are created with free wills, angels have the power to choose between good and evil. The angels who sinned did so, not by seeking evil rather than good, but by pursuing good in the wrong way—a way that manifested pride of self rather than love of God. That pride, according to Aquinas, can be understood as the desire on the part of Satan to be like God.

"He desired godlikeness," Aquinas writes, "in this sense, that he placed his ultimate bliss in an objective to be obtained by the force of his own nature alone, rejecting supernatural bliss, which depends on the grace of God." He wills to possess by the exercise of his natural powers what is attainable only by a willingness through love to be open to God's grace.

Aquinas then addresses himself to the following questions, all of which, except the first, he answers affirmatively.

Granted that no angel is evil by nature, could one of them have become evil, voluntarily, in the first instant of creation?

Granted that this was not possible, was there an interval between the creation and the fall of the first angel who sinned?

Was the highest angel who fell also the highest absolutely speaking?

Was the sin of the first sinful angel the cause of the others sinning?

His reason for a negative answer to the first question lies in the last verse of the first chapter of *Genesis*, in which God, surveying the world he created, regards it as good, very good. In that first instant, there is as yet no moral evil in it.

That is introduced in the very next instant by the sin of Satan, who was not only the highest angel that fell but also the highest of God's creatures, absolutely speaking. He was the cause of sin on the part of the other fallen angels, not by compelling them to sin, but by inducing them to do so.

The punishment of Satan and of the other angels who became devils with him consists in the darkening of their intellects—not through the loss of the knowledge that is connatural to them, but through the loss of the supernatural knowledge that is the gift of God's grace. Just as the blessed angels are confirmed in their bliss, so the devils are forever fixed in the punishment they merited by their wrongful choice.

To the question whether the punishment of the devils includes the suffering of pains, Aquinas responds by saying that, strictly speaking, the devils, being fallen angels and so purely spiritual creatures, cannot experience any sensible feelings or emotions, all of which are of bodily origin. But "something corresponding to them can be experienced by devils"; namely, the frustration of their will, which naturally desires the bliss of the beatific vision. This ultimate good they have lost by wishing to attain it without God's help. In other words, only the pain of loss or deprivation, not sensible pain, constitutes the punishment of the damned.

(2) *Satan in the Service of God*

Satan is God's adversary, but he is not pitted against God as an equal. To suppose that he confronts God as an equal and opposite force is akin to the teaching of the Manichaeans. It is the doctrine that St. Augustine succeeded in getting condemned as a Christian heresy.

Zoroastrianism, a Near Eastern religion that flourished in the ancient Persian Empire, involved a belief in two conflicting deities—Ahura Mazda, the principle of goodness, and Ahriman, the principle of evil. They opposed each other as equals in their struggle to control the world and influence the course of human life. The religion that was founded by Manes (or Manis) and that bears his name incorporated this duality of divinities into an amalgam that looked to Zoroaster, Buddha, and Jesus as its major prophets and that spread through the ancient world as a very influential sect of Christianity.

It was popular in the Roman Empire at the time of Augustine's youth. He tells us in his *Confessions* that he was attracted by the teachings of Faustus, a bishop of the Manichaean sect, and that he almost became a disciple. The materialistic view of the universe and of the Divine forces operating in it, which characterized Manichaeanism, proved comforting to Augustine who, in his early years, had difficulty with the notion of purely spiritual beings.

The preaching of St. Ambrose on the text "The letter killeth; the spirit giveth life" rescued him from his literal reading of the New Testament and, with the help of Plato, he overcame his earlier incomprehension of the spiritual. When, after his conversion to Christianity, he became Bishop of Hippo in North Africa and one of the leading theologians of his day, he wrote a powerful tract against the errors of the Manichaeans that led to its condemnation as a heresy by a church council in the fourth century A.D.

The orthodox view that displaced it declared Satan, the Prince of Darkness, to be subservient in all things to the will of God— not only subservient but also an instrument of Divine providence. In the *Book of Job*, the Lord asks Satan:

Have you considered my servant Job, that there is none like him on earth, a blameless and upright man, who fears God and turns away from evil?

Satan replies:

Does Job fear God for nought? Hast thou not put a hedge about him and his house and all that he has, on every side? Thou hast blessed the work of his hands and his possessions have increased in the land. But put forth thy hand now, and touch all that he has and he will curse thee to thy face.

Whereupon the Lord said to Satan: "Behold, all that he has is in your power; only upon himself do not put forth your hand."

Thus charged by God to try the faith of Job, Satan afflicted him with many miseries, which sorely perplexed Job in view of his blamelessness, but which did not ultimately turn him away from God. The story of Job's trials, quandaries, and resolution have been subject over the centuries to many interpretations, but they center on the significance of earthly rewards and punishments, not on the role that Satan plays in the drama. The archenemy of the Lord acts, with respect to Job, solely as God's agent, not as an independent force.

In Goethe's *Faust*, there is a Prologue in heaven in which Mephistopheles (another name for Satan) makes a wager with God that he can lead Faust astray, but only, he says to the Lord, "if you will give me your permission to lead him gentle on the path I choose." God grants permission on the same condition that he imposed upon Satan in the *Book of Job*:

> As long as on the earth he [Faust] shall survive,
> So long you'll meet no prohibition.
> Man errs as long as he doth survive.
>
> . . . If you can lay hold on him, you may
> Conduct him downward on your course.
> And stand abashed when you are forced to say:
> A good man, though his striving be obscure,
> Remains aware that there is one right way.

To say that the devil has an irresistible power to cause sin is to deny that human sin, original and subsequent, proceeds from the exercise of free choice on the part of Adam and his descendants. The theologian does not make this error. The devil, he holds, is "a cause of sin neither directly, nor sufficiently, but only by persuasion" to which some men, but not all, succumb.

Man's free will is inviolable even by God. Human beings would have no moral responsibility for sinning if their disobedience to the Divine law were caused by God instead of being an act of free will on their part. Neither God nor Satan is the cause of moral evil in the realm of human action, but Satan and the demons under his command bring pressure to bear upon the human will through incitement of the passions that can divert it from the good. This can happen only if man's will does not have the strength to resist the temptations aroused by wrong objects of desire.

Man's inner life is the battlefield whereon the temptations of the devil are opposed by the guardian angels appointed by God to protect men from their incitement. Devils, the theologian declares, "are not *sent* by God to attack men but are sometimes *permitted* to do so according to God's just decrees." To which he adds:

So that the contest should not be an unequal one, men get some compensation through the help of God's grace; and, second, through the guardianship of the [good] angels.

Tempting men is the special vocation of the devil. He tempts by arousing fleshly desires and the lust for wordly goods. The traditional triad of "the world, the flesh, and the devil" names the sources of temptation before it names the tempter who uses them to subvert man's will.

To the question, whether all sins can be attributed to the temptations aroused by the devil, the theologian responds by saying that the devil is indirectly the cause of all human sin "because he instigated the first man to sin and it was from this sin that there resulted a proneness to sin in the whole human race."

On the other hand, the devil is not the primary cause of any sin, since man is always free to resist temptations no matter what their strength or source. Nor is the devil even a contributing cause in every sinful act for, as the theologian points out, "not all sins are committed at the devil's instigation." Some are committed by free choice without any inducement from the devil, but simply from the weakness of the flesh.

(3) *The Mystery of Original Sin*

According to orthodox Christian doctrine, there are two origins of sin—two original sins—and they are not unrelated. One is the sin of Satan; the other, the sin of Adam. God is the cause of neither, for the creation of both Satan and Adam with free will puts the responsibility for sinning upon them, not upon their creator.

Both original sins are extremely difficult to understand. This the theologian frankly confesses. In their incomprehensibility by us lies the mystery that confronts us when we consider them.

Of the two, the sin of Satan is the more mysterious, for in Adam's fall, Satan operates as an instigator—a contributing, but not a determining, cause. But in Satan's fall there is no cause other than the free choice of the sinner.

In the essay on Satan referred to earlier, the writers point out that we are here confronted with "evil in its purest condition: the choice of a mind hitherto absolutely innocent, utterly unclouded by sentiment." Given the angel's natural love of God, whereby he loves himself only *because* of God, how could "aversion from God—that is, sin—occur?" To sin, the angel must prefer himself to God. "But such self-preference," the writers say, "does not seem possible."

To apprehend what is so difficult to understand about original sin, it may be helpful to recall the theologian's observation that, from Adam's original sin, "there resulted a proneness to sin in the whole human race." This proneness derives from the weakness of the human reason and will as a consequence of the wound inflicted upon human nature by original sin. Thus weakened, man's reason and will cannot, without God's healing grace, overcome the seductions of the world and the flesh and the temptations of the devil.

Before Adam sinned in the earthly Paradise, he was, according to the theologian, in a state of innocence, comparable to that of Satan at creation. His sensual appetites were subject to complete control by his reason and his will. But when he disobeyed God, he lost his innocence. His animal nature ceased to be subservient to his rational nature.

So long as Adam's will remained in harmony or concord with God's will, harmony reigned within Adam himself. His animal appetites were completely submissive to the rule of reason. But once his wrong choice brought him into discord with God, discord was introduced into his own nature.

The consequence of Adam's original sin is manifested in the conflictful nature inherited by all his descendants. As the theologian views it, the conflict between rationality and animality that is inherent in human nature is not only peculiar to man; it is also man's inheritance from Adam's original sin.

Given the conflict within themselves with which human beings must contend, it is understandable how they often choose that which appears good to them because their appetites crave it, even though their reason admonishes them that it is not really good for them. In the struggle between reason and the promptings of fleshly or worldly desires to act contrary to reason's recommendations, reason often loses out and the individual freely makes a choice that turns out to be wrong.

Sinning, from the theologian's point of view, is even more serious than an ordinary wrong choice. It turns man away from God and from man's ultimate supernatural good, not merely the good that befits his nature in this temporal life. If fallen man's wounded and conflictful nature explains his proneness to ordinary wrong-doing, how much more readily does it account for his proneness to sin.

The explanation that the theologian can give for the sins of mankind after the expulsion of the human race from the Garden of Eden is not available to him when he tries to understand original sin—the sin of Satan or of Adam.

Being a purely spiritual being, a mind without a body, Satan has an intellect and will that are unopposed by contrary inclinations within his nature. Knowledge of God is implanted in his created nature; love of God, in his created will. His will, of course, remains free to choose, but what is the option that presents itself for choice?

The theologian's answer to this question rests on a distinction between the knowledge of God that is implanted in Satan's created nature and God's knowledge of himself. More perfect than the natural knowledge of God possessed by any other angel, Satan's natural knowledge is still less perfect than God's knowledge of himself. Supernatural knowledge of God's essence is enjoyed only in the vision of God. This constitutes the bliss or beatitude that is conferred by God's grace and cannot be attained in any other way.

With this in mind, the theologian's explanation of Satan's sin then runs along the following lines. So near to God, with a nature filled with the knowledge of God, Satan desired more—the supernatural knowledge whereby God knows himself. This was tantamount to wishing to be God, or at least like God.

This desire or wish on Satan's part could have been gratified by a willingness on his part to have it fulfilled by God's grace. But, the theologian tells us, his pride—his love of self—made him reject the gift of grace. Loving himself more than he loved God, he wished to attain without God's grace what is attainable only through it. What he desired was good, not evil; but he sought to achieve the good in the wrong way.

The mystery still remains. The love that God implanted in the will of all angels at their creation conforms, as we noted earlier, to the first precept of charity. By such connatural love, all angels, including Satan, love God before they love themselves. How, then, could Satan have been so prideful in self-love that he committed the sin of preferring his own way to God's way, thus seeking to attain his ultimate good without God's help instead of being humble enough to receive it as a gift from God?

If there is an answer to this question, I cannot find it in dogmatic theology. Nor can I find an answer to the question how Adam could have committed original sin. The fact that he was tempted by Eve at the instigation of Satan does not explain his free decision to yield to that temptation instead of obeying God.

Just as Satan and other angels were created with the love of God implanted in their wills, so Adam was created, the theologian tells us, with a preternatural grace that implanted harmony in the rational animality of his nature. So long as this harmony prevailed, the animal part of his nature remained completely subservient to his reason and will.

His original sin, therefore, cannot be like ordinary human sinning, the result of a proneness to sin that is inherent in a conflictful nature. Adam did not yield to the seductions of Eve as we yield to the temptations of the flesh.

In reaching for what God forbade him to seek—the knowledge of good and evil which would make him like God—his choice paralleled the choice made by Satan. It, too, was an expression of pride—of self-love transcending love of God. He wanted his own way rather than God's.

But why? No answer is forthcoming. In the inscrutability of Satan's and of Adam's choice lies the mystery of original sin, and, indeed, the mystery of evil.

PART THREE

Angels as Objects of Philosophical Thought

7

The Possibility of Angels

(1) *The Crux of the Matter*

IF WE COULD not be assured that angels are at least possible beings—that it is possible for minds to exist without bodies—much, if not all, of what has been said about them so far would be nullified and nothing more could be said.

Religious belief in angels would be rendered absurd. The rational explanation of that belief, it will be recalled, involves an affirmation of the possibility of spiritual creatures. A created universe that did not include them would have failed to realize an important range of possibilities. The reality of angels is that realization.

Theological reasoning about the existence of God attempts to prove that God really exists. Theological reasoning about the reality of angels does not try to prove their existence; but, assuming that they belong in the realm of the possible, it offers a rational explanation of an article of religious faith—the belief in their reality. If it is impossible for angels to exist, all of this goes up in smoke, and with it the religious belief it tries to explain.

So much for looking backward on the steps we have taken so far. Turning now from religion and theology and looking forward to what philosophy can contribute to the discussion, we find our path blocked. To proceed philosophically, we do not need to affirm that angels really exist. There is much to be said about them as possibilities, much that has great philosophical significance. But nothing at all, if they are impossible.

[99]

Some philosophers have thought that a tenable and cogent argument for the reality of angels can be constructed. Examination of it reveals why it fails.

The argument rests on the following premises: (a) that God, the supreme being, not only exists, but is supremely good—good in the moral sense of that term; (b) that God's supreme goodness necessitates his creation of the best of all possible worlds; (c) that, since angels are among the possibilities to be realized, a universe in which they were missing would not be the best of all possible worlds. Hence, the reasoning concludes, God could not have created the best of all possible worlds without creating spiritual creatures as well as corporeal things.

The first of these premises, as I have tried to show in *How to Think About God*, goes beyond philosophy's power to affirm. The affirmation of God's existence is philosophically tenable, but not the affirmation of God's moral goodness. That is an article of religious faith.

The second premise not only goes beyond philosophy's reach. In addition, it is theologically questionable that God is under the necessity to create the best of all possible worlds.

With the first and second premises eliminated, we are left with a crucial clause in the third premise—the statement that "angels are among the possibilities to be realized." Whether or not they are realized in the universe that now exists; whether or not this universe is created by God; and whether or not, if created, it is the best of all the possible worlds within God's power to create; the statement that they are at least possible remains for us to consider.

In addition, it is a proposition about which philosophers disagree. Some affirm it; some deny it.

In the year during which I was engaged in preparing to write this book, almost everyone I told about the book in process popped two questions at me. "Do you believe in angels?" followed by "How many can stand on the head of a pin?"

At first I brushed these questions aside by saying that they were inappropriate to ask a philosopher. That proved to be an unsatisfactory response. The frequency of the questions finally led me to develop carefully formulated answers.

To the first I replied by saying that religious Jews, Christians, and Muslims believe that angels really exist, but that I, writing as a philosopher and a pagan, was concerned only with the possibility of their real existence. I then went on to explain why I was concerned with this question: first, because affirming the possibility of minds without bodies is indispensable to the credibility of the religious dogma about the existence of angels; and, second, because that possibility is itself a disputed question in philosophy. It is one that has serious consequences for many other matters of great philosophical interest.

To the second question about the number of angels that can dance on the head of a pin, I felt compelled to inform my questioners that that problem had never occupied the attention of a single thinker in the Middle Ages when angelology was so fully developed. Nor was it among the disputed questions that scholastic theologians and philosophers have been traditionally supposed to wrestle with in endless—and fruitless—debate.

So far as religious beliefs go concerning the mission that angels perform on earth at God's behest, dancing on the head of a pin is not one of them. The myth that intense discussion focussed on the number of angels that might dance on a pinhead is simply one of the many modern inventions contrived to make a mockery of mediaeval thought.

Having dismissed this venerable piece of modern nonsense, I then pointed out that a serious question remained and that it was one a philosopher can and should answer. Angels being bodiless, how many can be present at a given location in physical space—a place occupied by a body such as a human being, with regard to whom an angel might have a mission to perform?

The reason why that question cannot be avoided and the reason why the answer to it must be "Only one" will be made clear in the next chapter where I will undertake to explore the philosophical consequences of affirming that purely spiritual beings—minds without bodies—are genuinely possible.

In the Middle Ages, almost all of the great philosophers were also theologians—Jewish, Christian, or Muslim. The treatises on angels which they wrote did not sharply distinguish, on the one hand, questions that belong strictly to the sacred or dogmatic theologian alone (because asking and answering them cannot be undertaken except on the basis of texts to be found in Sacred Scriptures) and, on the other hand, questions that belong to the philosopher quite apart from theology (because asking and answering them in no way depends on Sacred Scriptures or Divine revelation).

In modern times, not many philosophers of eminence—philosophers who are not also engaged in the work of sacred theology—have given much thought to angels. Since the eighteenth century, there have been almost none except philosophers who also happened to be imbued with profound respect for the tenets of sacred theology. But in the sixteenth and seventeenth centuries, two noteworthy English philosophers—Francis Bacon and John Locke—not only affirmed the possibility of angels, but also regarded the consideration of the possibility a proper subject for purely philosophical discourse.

In Bacon's *Advancement of Learning*, which he wrote as a survey of the whole realm of human inquiry and as an appraisal of future progress therein, he maintains that it is improper for philosophers "from the contemplation of nature and the principle of human reason, to dispute or urge anything with vehemence as to the mysteries of faith." But it is not inappropriate, he declares, for philosophers to consider "the nature of spirits and angels; this being neither unsearchable nor forbid, but in a great part level to the human being on account of their affinity."

Bacon does not further instruct us concerning angels in the *Advancement of Learning,* but he does make one further point about them in his *Novum Organum,* his treatise on the methods to be followed in scientific and philosophical inquiry. There, in the context of developing his theory of induction, Bacon denies that the human mind has the power to ascend at once from particular experiences to the most universal forms that inhere in things. Human induction should proceed gradually from the less to the more universal. "It is only for God (the bestower and creator of forms)," he writes, "and perhaps also for angels or intelligences at once to recognize such supremely universal forms at the first glance of contemplation."

John Locke's consideration of angels—or spiritual substances—is both more extensive and more argumentative than Bacon's. It is a matter of prime importance in his *Essay Concerning Human Understanding*, especially in those parts of his essay that deal with the scope and validity of human knowledge. In addition, Locke engages in dispute with those who would deny the bare possibility that purely spiritual substances can exist, quite apart from the question whether in fact they really do. He advances what, in my opinion, are persuasive arguments in support of the proposition that minds without bodies are as possible—and as intelligible to us—as bodies without minds.

I will postpone the consideration of his and other arguments to this effect until after we have examined the views of those who insist that purely spiritual beings are simply impossible.

(2) *Who Says That Angels Are Impossible?*

Who, indeed? The materialists—those who assert that nothing exists except bodies, corporeal substances occupying physical space by their extension or bulk.

The atomists of antiquity—Leucippus and Democritus in Greece and their Roman disciple, Epicurus, whose views are celebrated in the great philosophical poem by Lucretius, *On the Nature of Things*—laid it down as their basic tenet that nothing exists except atoms and the void, the empty space in which atoms move about.

This central tenet of ancient atomism was espoused in modern times by Thomas Hobbes, whose views about the impossibility of angels we shall examine in a moment. Locke had Hobbes in mind in his effort to refute what he regarded as a dogmatic denial of spiritual substances.

Since the sixteenth century, materialism has become a much more sophisticated philosophical doctrine than that of atomism in either its ancient or its modern form. The notion of the atom as an absolutely indivisible unit of matter has been replaced by conceptions of the atom as a complex structure comprised of more elementary particles. Their divisibility or indivisibility does not affect the central tenet of the more sophisticated forms of materialism, which still declare that nothing exists except bodies.

Even when it is conceded that mental processes cannot be reduced to physical processes—that acts of the mind are distinguishable from the action of the brain—it is still stoutly maintained that mental acts do not occur independently of brain states. Just as seeing or hearing do not occur without the action of eyes or ears, so thinking does not occur without the action of the brain.

To concede, as the more moderate materialists do, that thinking is at least analytically distinguishable from brain action, is not, in their view, inconsistent with regarding brain action as both a necessary and a sufficient condition for thinking or any other act of mind.

Only the most extreme materialists, now generally discredited, persist in rejecting even an analytical distinction between mental and physical processes, regarding them as so completely identical as to be indistinguishable.

The notion of angels—of minds totally devoid of bodies—is anathema to materialists of every variety, atomistic or not, extreme or moderate. The gist of their argument runs as follows.

(i) Nothing exists except corporeal things, whether these be atoms, elementary particles of matter or units of energy, or complex bodies somehow constituted by these simpler components.

(ii) Angels are said to be incorporeal beings, minds without bodies, purely spiritual substances.

Therefore, angels—spiritual substances—do not exist.

Let us for the moment grant the truth of the first premise. The truth of the second premise is beyond question. From these two truths, the conclusion inexorably follows. It cannot be avoided or denied.

But what does that conclusion assert? That angels, spiritual substances, minds without bodies, *do not really exist?* Or that they *cannot exist*—that they are *impossible?* On the face of it, the former, and only the former.

From the assertion that nothing actually exists except corporeal things and from the acceptance of the statement that the word "angel" is here used to refer to something totally incorporeal, the only conclusion that can be validly drawn is that the word "angel" refers to nothing that actually exists. The premises certainly do not support the conclusion that the word "angel" refers to something which is intrinsically impossible and, therefore, the word "angel" is totally devoid of meaning.

Yet it is precisely this conclusion that Thomas Hobbes did in fact draw from his materialistic premises.

In his book *The Leviathan,* Hobbes did not deny the reality of angels, for that would have involved him in rejecting the testimony of Sacred Scriptures. However, he interprets the scriptural passages in which their earthly visitations are described by saying that they are "nothing but supernatural apparitions of the fancy, raised by the special and extraordinary operation of God, thereby to make His presence and commandments known to mankind, and chiefly to His own people."

As for the existence of angels quite apart from such earthly visitations in various bodily forms, Hobbes insists that if angels are supposed to have permanent being, then they must be corporeal.

Why? Because, according to Hobbes, the very notion of an incorporeal substance is as self-contradictory as is the notion of a round square. Anyone who understands the signification of these words "substance" and "incorporeal," and who also understands the word "incorporeal" to mean "having no body at all, not just a subtle body," should be able to see at once that these two words taken together "imply a contradiction."

Hobbes's argument holds for "round square," but not for "incorporeal substance." The phrase "round square" is on the very face of it self-contradictory. Being self-contradictory, it refers to nothing that is thinkable—to no possible object of thought.

To recognize that "round square" is a self-contradictory form of speech is to recognize more than that round squares *do not* really exist. Round squares *cannot* exist either in reality or as objects of thought. The phrase "round square" is, therefore, truly meaningless. It refers to nothing at all.

The same argument would apply to the phrase "incorporeal substances" or to the phrase "spiritual being" if—*and only if*—the meaning of the word "substance" is identical with the meaning of the word "body" or if—*and only if*—the meaning of the word "being" is inseparable from the meaning of the word "physical" or "corporeal." But, as I will try to show in the following section, that is not the case. Neither our understanding of substance nor our understanding of being so entails the notions of corporeality or physical existence that the phrases "incorporeal substance" or "spiritual being" become self-contradictory in the way in which "round square" is.

If words or phrases that do not refer to anything that actually exists in reality must be regarded as totally meaningless because of that fact, it would be impossible for us ever to ask whether something we are able to think about does in fact exist. The phrase "round square" being self-contradictory, we do not ask whether round squares really exist. Precisely because the phrase "incorporeal substance" or "spiritual being" is not self-contradictory, we can and do ask the question whether angels—minds without bodies—really exist.

The materialist may be correct in his denial of the reality of angels, or of minds independent of bodies. Whether or not he is correct depends upon the truth of his basic premise that nothing really exists except corporeal substances or bodies.

This premise, to say the least, is philosophically questionable. It is certainly not self-evidently true; nor has any cogent demonstration of its truth ever been advanced. This is not to say that it must be rejected as false, but only to say that the conclusions of the materialist rest upon an assumption open to question.

The materialist assumption that spiritual substances do not exist is as much an act of faith as the religious belief in the reality of angels. The latter is an act of religious faith; the former, it might be said, is an act of anti-religious faith. But, with one or two notable exceptions, the religious faith in the existence of spiritual beings is not ordinarily accompanied by the denial of material things or by the notion that bodies are impossible.

The denial of reality to angels is one thing; the denial of their possibility is quite another. The materialist assumption that nothing really exists except bodies or corporeal substances does not render the phrase "incorporeal substance" or the phrase "spiritual being" self-contradictory or meaningless. It does not, therefore, lead to the conclusion that angels are impossible.

They remain possible as objects of thought about which we can meaningfully ask whether or not they really exist; i.e., exist independently of our thinking about them. And if the fundamental tenet of materialism—the questionable assumption on which the doctrine rests—turns out to be false, the religious belief in the reality of angels may be true. Whether or not that is the case, good reasons can be given for rejecting the materialist's denial of their possibility.

(3) *Reasons for Affirming Their Possibility*

One reason has already emerged. The fact that materialism—the philosophical doctrine most antagonistic to the notion of spiritual beings—provides no grounds for denying the possibility of such beings is a negative approach to affirming their possibility. To acknowledge that we have no reason for thinking angels impossible is tantamount to conceding that they are possible.

Can we go beyond this and find positive reasons for an affirmative conclusion?

St. Thomas Aquinas pointed out that the failure to acknowledge the possibility of spiritual beings stems from the failure to distinguish between sense-perception and imagination, on the one hand, and intellection or understanding, on the other. This failure led some philosophers to the conclusion that nothing exists or can exist except that which can be sensed and imagined. Since nothing is perceptible or imaginable other than bodies, these philosophers concluded that only bodies exist or can exist.

Both Plato and Aristotle, Aquinas observed, corrected this error on the part of earlier philosophers. They both recognized a realm of intelligible objects—objects of thought, quite distinct and separate from a realm of sensible objects—objects of perception and imagination. Corresponding to that distinction, they recognize that man has two distinct powers of apprehending objects: on the one hand, the sensitive powers that man shares with other animals; on the other hand, the intellectual powers that only human beings possess.

Intelligible objects or objects of thought are not apprehended as bodies or as having bodily attributes. On the contrary, they are apprehended devoid of all corporeal or material characteristics. That such immaterial objects exist as objects of thought does not lead to the conclusion that they also exist in reality, quite apart from human thought, but it does at least permit us to affirm the possibility of their existence.

A second reason advanced by Aquinas for thinking that minds without bodies are possible is the view he held concerning the human intellect and its action. Adopting Aristotle's analysis of man's powers, Aquinas maintained that all but one of these are corporeal powers, the actions of which are the actions of bodily organs.

According to this view, digestion is the act of the organs of the alimentary system; locomotion, the act of the skeletal and muscular systems; sensing, the act of the sense organs and brain; imagining, the act of the brain when the senses are not in operation. But intellection—understanding and thinking—is not correspondingly the act of the brain. It is the act of an incorporeal power that man possesses.

Neither Aristotle nor Aquinas supposed that we can understand or think without that activity being accompanied by the activity of the brain. They both recognized the effect upon our power to think of brain injuries, of drugs, and of the fatigue poisons that cause sleep. However, to admit that we cannot think or understand without using the brain is not to say that we think or understand simply by using the corporeal organ that is primarily an organ of sense-perception, sensory imagination, and sensory memory.

The moderate materialist, as we have seen, regards brain action as *both* a necessary and a sufficient condition for all mental processes, whether these are sensory or intellectual; but he does not *identify* mental processes with the processes of the brain and nervous system. He recognizes that they are distinguishable. Each has properties not possessed by the other.

It would, therefore, appear quite appropriate to call Aristotle and Aquinas moderate immaterialists. They do not go to the extreme of asserting that a mind that is associated with a human body has the power to think and understand in and of itself, without dependence on any bodily organ. In contrast to such extreme immaterialism, their view is that the action of the brain and nervous system is a necessary, but *not a sufficient*, condition for understanding and thinking. The action of the human intellect—in their view, an incorporeal power, a power not seated in a bodily organ—is required for understanding or thinking to occur.

Here, then, we have another argument for the possibility of minds without bodies—intellects not associated with bodies as the human intellect is. Affirming man's possession of an intellect that is an incorporeal power, moderate immaterialists, such as Aristotle and Aquinas, see no obstacle whatsoever to affirming the possibility of intellects superior to the human intellect, superior precisely because they are totally divorced from bodies.

There is still a fourth view to consider—that of the seventeenth-century French philosopher, Descartes. His theory of the human mind is that it is, in and of itself, a thinking substance—a *res cogitans*. It is associated with the human body, which is an utterly different kind of substance, a *res extensa* or extended substance, having the tridimensionality of physical bulk.

Let us ignore for the moment all the well-nigh insoluble difficulties of the so-called "mind-body problem" that arise from the association in one individual of two such disparate substances. I will return to them later. Here we need only note two things.

The first is that the Cartesian view completes the picture by being the extreme immaterialism that lies at the other end of the line from the extreme materialism that totally identifies mental with physical processes. In between these two extremes are the two moderate views that I have described as moderate materialism and moderate immaterialism.

The second point is what follows from the Cartesian affirmation of the existence in the human individual of an intellect that is a thinking substance, not only distinct from, but also separate in its existence and operation from, the extended substance that is the human body. Holding that to be the case, the Cartesian doctrine does not hesitate to embrace the possibility of there being minds totally divorced from bodies.

In fact, on the Cartesian view, the existence of such completely separated thinking substances is less difficult to understand than the existence of the human mind that, while separate in its existence from a body, is nevertheless associated with one—inexplicably.

In one of the *Objections and Replies* attached to his *Meditations*, Descartes tells us that from the ideas we possess of God and of man, especially our idea of the human intellect as a thinking substance, we have no difficulty whatsoever in forming the ideas of angels as pure intelligences—thinking substances not in any way associated with bodies, as human intellects are.

Certainly, any philosopher who, on rational grounds, affirms the real existence of God can affirm, not the actual existence of angels, but the possibility of their existing. One qualification must be added to the foregoing statement; namely, that the God whose existence is affirmed must be understood to be not only the supreme being, uncaused and unconditioned, but also a purely spiritual and infinite being.

Even to ask the question whether such a being really exists presupposes the acknowledgment of the possibility of its existence. As much as the theist who affirms, the atheist who denies makes this acknowledgment. Atheism, in all its forms, does not deny the possibility, but only the actuality of God.

So, too, the agnostic denies only the knowability of God—our being able to know by reason God's existence or attributes. The agnostic does not deny that God is thinkable by us—that we can form the notion of a purely spiritual being, having an existence that is independent of the existence of anything else.

If the possibility of there being a God, or of our being able to ask whether or not God exists, rests on our being able to think of God without self-contradiction, then, *a fortiori*, the same reasoning applies to angels—purely spiritual beings that are finite rather than infinite. Unlike God, if these finite spiritual beings do really exist, they exist dependently, not independently. Their existence depends upon their being created by God and sustained in existence by God.

A metaphysical insight underlies all the arguments advanced so far in support of the affirmation that God and angels are at least possible beings. It has two ingredients.

One is the conception of a substance as anything having an existence separate from the existence of everything else, even though its existence may interact with or be related to the existence of other things. An atom, a stone, a tree, a horse, a human being—each is a substance in this sense of the term. The atom's weight, the stone's shape, the tree's height, the horse's color, and the human being's talents are not substances. They are attributes of the substances to which they belong. They do not have any existence separate from the existence of the substance of which they are attributes.

The second element involved in the underlying metaphysical insight is the recognition that the various physical dimensions or properties that comprise the characteristics of corporeal substances are accidental rather than essential attributes of substance itself.

This is tantamount to saying that while this or that physical attribute may be necessarily present as a property of corporeal substances, it is not necessarily present in all substances. The notion of substance does not necessarily involve the possession of such attributes.

Therefore, it follows that incorporeal substances, such as angels or minds without bodies, can exist without having the physical attributes possessed by corporeal substances.

To see that this is so is to see that purely spiritual substances—God, angels, or minds without bodies—are possible modes of being.

There remains only to add the contribution made by John Locke to the discussion of this subject. In his *Essay Concerning Human Understanding,* he dwells at length and in many places on the comparable intelligibility of corporeal and incorporeal substances. He is at pains to point out all the difficulties that confront us in dealing with the notion of substance as that underlying substratum in which attributes inhere. But our difficulties, he declares, are no greater in the case of spirits, or incorporeal substances, than in the case of bodies, or corporeal substances.

The fact that the attributes of bodies are perceptible by our senses, whereas the attributes of spirits are not, does not make spiritual substances any less intelligible to us than corporeal substances. The fact that we can know the existence of corporeal substances directly by sense-perception, whereas we have no such immediate knowledge of the existence of spiritual substances, does not affect either the intelligibility or the possibility of the latter.

The possibility of angels, or minds without bodies, being thus explained as something we need not hesitate to affirm, philosophy is called upon to explore that possibility. Granted that angels are possible beings, what more can be said about them by the philosopher proceeding, as he should, without any light drawn from Divine revelation or from articles of religious faith?

8

Philosophical Exploration of That Possibility

(1) *Angelology and Mathematics*

AN UNLIKELY affinity, yet angelology and mathematics are
two forms of human inquiry that are concerned with ideal objects or objects in the realm of the possible, as opposed to dealing
with really existent things.

Pure mathematics and philosophical angelology are further alike
in being works of the mind proceeding logically from a set of
initial premises. Neither engages in empirical investigation of any
sort; neither needs to resort to observations or experiments. Even
in the most perfectly constructed mathematical system, some
propositions will be found undecidable as to their truth or fal-
sity. So, too, in angelology there will be some unanswerable questions.

The similarities end there. The rigor of mathematical reasoning and the certitude that can often be attained in the establish-
ment of its conclusions cannot be matched in angelology. Some
of the conclusions to be reached may have a comparable certitude, but we will have to be satisfied with less assurance than
that in many cases.

It should be noted that what has just been said applies only to
philosophical angelology, not to angelology as a branch of sacred
or dogmatic theology. The initial premises or principles that
fix the framework within which philosophical inquiry concern-

ing angels proceeds include no articles of religious faith, no dogmatic declarations, and no references to the testimony of Sacred Scriptures.

None of the angelologies developed in the Middle Ages were philosophical in the manner just described. All were the work of dogmatic or sacred theologians. Nevertheless, it must also be observed that they often went beyond the bounds of sacred theology by raising questions about angels not prompted by any scriptural passages and by offering answers to them that had the character of philosophical speculation rather than that of attempts to provide a rational basis for articles of faith or an explanation of scriptural texts.

Some of the things said about angels that represent the results of philosophical speculation on the part of mediaeval theologians can be supported by reasoning from the very slim set of initial premises on which we will try to base our conclusions here. Some, however, will require us to make additional suppositions. And some are like the undecidable propositions in a consistently developed mathematical system. We will be able to find no basis for judging them to be either true or false.

What I have referred to as the slim set of initial premises that provide the grounds for philosophical reasoning about angels consists of a single definition, a single axiom, and a single postulate. They can be stated as follows:

Definition: As an object of thought, an angel is a purely spiritual being, an incorporeal substance, a mind without a body and one not associated with a body that is its own.

Axiom: An incorporeal substance is a possible mode of being.
Explication of the axiom:
The self-evident truth of the foregoing statement lies in the absence of self-contradiction in the conjunction of *substance* with *incorporeal*. What is self-contradictory is impossible. What is not is possible. To say that an angel is possible is to say that it can exist in reality whether or not it actually does exist.

Postulate: Let it be granted that, in the realm of the possible, there
is a multitude of incorporeal substances, a plurality of
angels.

Explication of the postulate:

Neither the definition nor the axiom requires that there
be many angels as objects of thought.

In postulating a plurality of angels, we are also assuming
that the incorporeal substances or spiritual beings we are
considering are finite, which is to say that each is limited
by the differences that must obtain among them if they
are many.

In other words, if angels as objects of thought and thus
as mere possibilities were also to have real existence, that
existence would be a finite and limited mode of existence.

The sparsity of this set of initial premises or principles is such
that we should expect a correspondingly sparse set of conclusions following from them. The scope of philosophical angelology, as compared with the scope of a theological treatise on
angels, is slim.

In *How to Think About God*, I called attention to a similar
contrast between philosophical and sacred theology. What can
be said by the philosopher about the attributes and actions of
the supreme being who is the deity believed in and worshiped
by the faithful is relatively slight as compared with what can be
said by the theologian who proceeds upon the basis of what he
accepts as God's revelation of himself in Sacred Scriptures.

The sacred theologian employs his reason to explain or understand religious beliefs that are articles of faith, not to prove
propositions about God on the basis of reason alone. The limited
scope of philosophical theology derives from the limitations imposed upon it by having to operate on the basis of unaided reason, drawing no light or inspiration from Divine revelation.

Though philosophical theology proceeds under the limitations
just stated, its procedure corresponds to that of sacred theology
in one very important respect. When we use words to say any-

thing positively or affirmatively about the attributes of God, and also use the same words to characterize the attributes or actions of the corporeal things we know as components of the physical reality of which we ourselves are a part, those words must be understood in an analogical rather than a univocal sense.

For example, when we say that God lives, knows, or loves, and also say of ourselves that we live, know, or love, the life, knowledge, or love signified when the reference is to God is not identical with the life, knowledge, or love signified when the reference is to us.

Our use of the words is neither univocal (carrying an identical signification in both uses) nor is it utterly equivocal (having no common significance at all in both uses).

To say that the significance is analogical rather than univocal or equivocal is to say that whatever sameness resides in the meaning of the word in its two applications is intrinsically diversified by the difference between the two subjects to which it is applied—God, an infinite and spiritual being, on the one hand, and us, finite and corporeal beings, on the other hand.

Only when what we say about God is negative, denying with respect to God what we affirm about us, are the words we use employed in a univocal sense. For example, when we say that God is infinite, incorporeal, independent, or uncaused in his existence, we are saying that God's existence is *not* finite, *not* corporeal, *not* dependent, *not* caused in the precise sense in which we, and all the other things of the world with which we have become acquainted in experience, are finite, corporeal, dependent, and caused.

In philosophical theology, as compared with sacred theology, most of the things we are able to say about God with clarity and assurance are negative rather than affirmative. Exempt from the limitations to which philosophical theology is subject, sacred theology is much richer, because Sacred Scriptures provide it with a basis for a much wider range of affirmative declarations about God.

All of these similarities and differences between philosophical and sacred theology should be observed with respect to an angelology that is purely philosophical and one that is the branch of sacred theology. With two exceptions, whatever we can say affirmatively about angels and human beings must be understood analogically.

The first exception is the statement expressed in our initial postulate—that angels, like us, have a finite, not an infinite, mode of being. The second is that an angel, conceived as a possible rather than as a necessary being, is not only capable of existing, but is also capable of not existing. We must, and do in fact, affirm the same thing of ourselves. Yet, even here, we must recognize that if angels exist in reality, their spiritual and our material existence are analogical modes of existence.

Whatever else we say affirmatively about attributes of angels—their knowledge or their love—must be said analogically, because the knowledge and love of minds without bodies cannot be the same as the knowledge and love of minds having bodies, which is our condition as corporeal, not incorporeal, substances.

One further point must be noted before we proceed with our philosophical exploration of the possibility of angels.

Some of the questions we shall consider in that exploration are categorical in character. This means that they can be asked and answered solely on the basis of the slim set of initial premises or principles laid down. As we shall see, the number of such questions will be few.

To go beyond these few categorical questions, we must resort to hypothetical questions. Such hypothetical questions require us to make additional suppositions—suppositions not included in or derivable from our initial definition, axiom, and postulate.

Making such suppositions allows the philosopher to stay within the realm of the merely possible. The "if" clause that introduces a hypothetical question asserts nothing as a matter of fact. It merely lays down a supposition that may or may not be contrafactual.

Consider, for example, the following hypothetical question:

"*If* angels really exist and *if* they have the power to act on bodies in the physical world, in what ways can they so act?" Asking such a hypothetical question does not involve us in asserting that angels actually exist in reality or that they do in fact act on bodies in the physical world. It merely envisages a possibility, and one that goes beyond anything stated in our initial set of premises.

Categorical questions about angels can be asked as well as answered on the basis of our initial premises and nothing more.

Hypothetical questions about angels cannot be asked without making additional suppositions, but they can be answered on the basis of our initial premises and nothing more.

Beyond these two types of questions about angels that a philosopher can ask and answer are questions that only a theologian can ask, some of which he can answer with assurance because he has scriptural warrant for doing so, and some of which he answers as a matter of opinion on his part, admitting the presence of conflicting opinions about the matter under consideration.

In responding to many questions about angels, Aquinas reports a diversity of opinion among theologians, usually indicating the opinion he himself espouses. In other cases, he argues for just one answer and attempts to rebut all the objections that can be raised against this answer.

In the following sections of this chapter, where the philosophically answerable questions are relatively few, I may sometimes conclude the section by summarizing opinions advanced in sacred theology, opinions that are assured or disputable. This will enlarge the discussion of the subject under consideration and may be of some interest to the reader.

(2) *The Mutability of Angels*

Corporeal things are mutable in one or more respects. They are susceptible to change of place. They are alterable in their qualities. They are subject to increase and decrease, to change in quantity. They come into being and pass away; that is, they are generable and perishable.

All corporeal things may not be subject to change in all of these respects, but none is exempt from change in one or more of these respects.

The mutability of corporeal things is inseparable from the temporal character of their existence. Anything that changes in any respect changes with the passage of time. Anything that is changeable in a certain respect, but remains unchanged, endures in that respect for a span of time.

Does our conception of angels as possible beings include mutability? Must we think of them as subject to change in any respect; and, if so, in what respect? Must we think of them as eternal and immutable beings like God or as changeable and temporal beings like us and other corporeal things?

In philosophical theology, we affirm eternity and immutability as attributes possessed only by the supreme being that is infinite and uncaused. Though the word "eternity" appears to be positive in its significance, it is in fact negative. Attributed to God, it negates temporality. The physical cosmos may have an everlasting existence, with neither beginning nor end, but it is not eternal because it is everlastingly subject to change in the course of everlasting time. To say that God is *not* changeable in any way is also to say that God does *not* exist in time (i.e., is eternal).

If only the supreme being is not subject to change, then angels, conceived as finite beings, cannot be totally exempt from change. If only the supreme being is eternal (in the sense of *not* existing in time), then angels cannot be conceived as eternal in that sense.

The question still remains to be answered more fully. Must angels be conceived as temporal beings in exactly the same way that we think of corporeal substances as temporal beings? Must we think of them as susceptible to change in all the respects in which we think of corporeal substances as susceptible to change?

The answer to be given to these questions is dictated by the difference between corporeal and incorporeal modes of being.

A corporeal substance, such as a human being, is composite of matter and form. It is a composite whole constituted by an organization of components parts or elements. That organization is the form inherent in its matter.

Whatever is composite in either of these ways is also decomposable. When we say that all human beings or all animals are mortal, we have in mind that they are decomposable and so perishable.

Being defined as incorporeal substances, as purely spiritual beings, angels are not thus decomposable. They cannot be generated as plants and animals are generated, nor can they perish as plants and animals do. The mortality that belongs by nature to all corporeal living things does not belong by nature to them.

Now let us ask two hypothetical questions. First, if angels really exist, are they created by God in the sense of having been brought into existence out of nothing, as the cosmos is said to have been brought into existence out of nothing when it is said to have been created by God? Second, if angels really exist, are they preserved in their existence by God in such wise that they would cease to exist if God ceased to preserve them in existence?

Our answer to the first of these questions must be like our answer to the question about the physical cosmos as a whole. In philosophical theology, we must assume that the physical cosmos does not have a beginning, for to assume the contrary would be tantamount to assuming that God exists as its creator. This would beg the question about God's existence which a philosophical theologian tries to answer.

For exactly the same reason, the hypothetical question that begins by assuming that angels really exist must be accompanied by the assumption that they have always existed—that, like the physical cosmos, they did not have a beginning by Divine creation. This is, of course, contrary to what is revealed in the first sentence of *Genesis*. Sacred theology must affirm the creation or initiation of both spiritual and corporeal beings, but philosophical theology cannot.

This brings us, then, to the second hypothetical question. If angels really exist, must their continuing existence be preserved by God?

An affirmative answer is dictated by the fact that we conceive angels as merely possible beings, capable of existing or not existing in reality. To think of them as incapable of not existing would be to think of them as necessary, not merely possible, beings.

The physical cosmos may exist everlastingly without beginning or end. So, too, the realm of spiritual beings—if such a realm actually exists—may exist everlastingly without beginning or end. But since both are merely possible beings, their continued existence requires a cause that preserves them in existence.

That preservative cause must be God, an infinite and uncaused being that, unlike any finite substance, corporeal or incorporeal, has the unique power to cause existence and nonexistence.

We must, therefore, think of angels as subject to change, at least to the extent that, if they do exist, they are capable of ceasing to exist. Their ceasing to exist would not be like the death of corporeal organisms through natural causes. Unlike corporeal organisms, which are by nature mortal, they are by nature immortal. However, their natural immortality does not preclude their supernatural annihilability—their ceasing to exist by God's ceasing to preserve them in existence.

Are angels subject to change in any other respect? Since they are immaterial, they are certainly not subject to change in exactly the same respects that material things are subject to change. Since they are minds, though without bodies, it may be thought that angels are subject to the kind of changes to which the human mind is susceptible.

It is necessary to qualify this last statement by immediately adding that whatever changes occur in the human mind as a result of its being associated with a human body, cannot occur in a mind that has no body. For example, the human mind changes from time to time in what it knows and understands by learning and growing in ways that are affected by sense-experience. Sense-experience involves the action of bodily organs. Hence, minds without bodies cannot learn and grow in this way.

Theologians go beyond anything a philosopher can say about the mutability of angels. As we observed in Chapter 5, two great thirteenth-century theologians, Aquinas and Bonaventure (one a Dominican and an Aristotelian; the other a Franciscan and a Platonist), advance conflicting opinions on the subject.

(3) *The Differentiation of Angels*

We have assumed that the possibility of angelic being includes the possibility of a plurality of angels. We are thereby compelled to ask how, in a multitude of possible angels, one angel differs from another.

In an attempt to answer this question, it will be helpful to consider the ways in which corporeal substances differ from one another. We can then inquire whether incorporeal substances differ in the same way.

Two physical things can differ in the species to which they belong. If both are members of the same species, they can differ as individuals. Specifically alike, they can differ individually in a number of ways.

For example in the physical realm, atoms that have the same weight and interior structure are specifically alike; atoms of different weights and interior structure are specifically different. Two atoms that are specifically alike are nevertheless two different individuals, two different members of the same species. Their individual difference or twoness consists in the fact that each occupies a different place or is at a different position in space.

In the domain of living organisms, individual differences are more complex. Two plants or two animals that are specifically alike differ as individuals in the following ways. First of all, they differ individually in the same way that two atoms that are specifically alike differ; namely, by the unique place or position that each occupies in space. In addition, they can differ by one's having certain accidental traits not possessed by the other.

For example, one rose of a certain species can be pink, another of the same species red. One man can have skin of light complexion; another, skin of dark complexion. In both examples, the color of the individual is an accidental quality in the sense that it in no way prevents the individuals, who thus differ, from belonging to the same species.

There is still a third way in which living organisms that belong to the same species differ as individual members of it. With regard to certain attributes which are not accidental traits as above, but rather are specific properties (i.e., attributes belonging to *every* member of the species), one individual may possess a given specific property to a greater or lesser degree than another.

If all roses of a certain species have thorns, one individual member of that species may have more thorns, or larger thorns, than another. All members of the human race have the property of being able to reason, but some individuals are better at it than others, whether through natural endowment or through acquired skill.

So much for individual differences among members of the same species. We must also distinguish between two ways in which individuals can differ specifically from one another. This requires us to consider a distinction between two ways in which the notion of species is employed—in one way by biological scientists; in another way by metaphysicians.

Aristotle was both a biological scientist and a metaphysician and, accordingly, employed the word "species" in both ways. In his biological treatises, wherein he set forth elaborate classifications of plants and animals, he used the notion of species in the same way that modern biological scientists use it.

Two species belonging to the same genus and, therefore, having the same generic traits may differ from one another by the first's having a trait or traits lacked by the second, and the second possessing a trait or traits lacked by the first. The two species differing in this manner are coordinate with one another as members of the same genus.

In his *Metaphysics* and his treatise *On the Soul*, Aristotle employed a quite different notion of species. There he said that two species are never coordinate; one is always higher or lower than the other by virtue of the fact that the higher of the species possesses all the specific properties present in the lower and possesses, in addition, one or more specific properties not possessed by the lower.

Thus, for example, an animal organism has all the vital vegetative powers that are specifically present in plants. In addition, it has certain powers such as sensation and locomotion that are specifically present only in animals. So, too, human beings have all the properties present in the two inferior species of living organisms—the vital powers of plants and of subhuman animals. Human beings differ specifically from the other two species of organisms by also having rational and intellectual powers not possessed by them.

This metaphysical account of species and specific differences led Aristotle to compare the ordering of species to the order that exists among whole numbers or integers and the order that exists among the regular polygons in plane geometry.

In both cases, the order consists of a discontinuous sequence. In the sequence of whole numbers, there is nothing between 1 and 2 or 2 and 3. In the sequence of regular polygons, there is no three-and-a-half sided figure between triangles and quadrangles.

In both cases, the difference between any two proximate members of the sequence is plus or minus one. The higher integer or polygon is plus one; the lower, minus one. Correspondingly, the difference between two proximate species of living organisms is that the higher has all the properties inseparable from membership in the lower species plus one property or one set of related properties not possessed by the lower.

Using this metaphysical notion of species, Aristotle was not able to find more than three species of living organisms. But using the notion of species that is employed in biological science, he named and classified hundreds upon hundreds, up to many thousands. Modern botanical and zoological classifications go much further, naming and arranging millions of plants and animal species.

We are now prepared to ask whether (a) the differences between angels are always specific and never individual differences, or (b) both specific and individual differences; and (c) if specific, in which sense of the term *specific*—the metaphysical or the biological sense.

We can say at once that two angels cannot differ individually as two atoms or any other two bodies differ—by the difference between the unique places or positions each occupies in space. Except when, in performing their earthly missions, angels act on terrestrial bodies, they do not occupy space. In Heaven, two angels may be in different positions relative to one another, but these positions must be understood as spiritually different, not as different places.

It has been supposed that the matter which enters into the composition of any corporeal substance is the one and only source of its individuality. The other element in the composite is the form or principle of organization. This must be the same in all members of the same species. It, therefore, necessarily follows that incorporeal substances cannot differ individually from one another in any of the ways in which two corporeal substances of the same species differ individually from one another.

Having no bodies and not being composite of matter and form, it is impossible, on the supposition just stated, for two angels to be individually different members of the same species. It must follow that each angel is a distinct species differing from another angel as one species differs from another.

One aspect of the question remains to be answered. Granted that angels differ only as species differ, not as individuals differ, we must ask: According to which theory of species do they differ—the scientific or the philosophical theory of species that determines how species are differentiated from and ordered to one another?

Nothing that we have learned about angels so far enables us to answer this question. However, what will be learned (in Section 5, to follow) concerning the knowledge and understanding of angels dictates an answer. There it will be seen that angels are differentiated by the number of innate ideas each has and by the comprehensiveness of these ideas, with the result that each angel is higher or lower than another.

If there are no two angels of equal rank, even when they belong to the same generic class of angels, then it follows that the order of the angelic species is like the order of whole numbers or of regular polygons, or like the order Aristotle assigned to the three species of living organisms—plants, brute animals, and human or rational animals.

Even when a number of angels, differing as species differ, belong to the same generic class of angels, their being ordered as inferior and superior rather than as coordinate and equal species in a genus signifies that it is the metaphysical, not the scientific, notion of species that applies to angels.

We have come this far on the basis of a supposition stated a few pages back. Two great mediaeval theologians and philosophers, St. Thomas Aquinas and St. Bonaventure, do not agree about the truth of the supposition laid down. According to Bonaventure, physical matter, corporeality, or having a body is not the sole or indispensable cause of individual differences. He maintained, therefore, contrary to Aquinas, that it is not impossible for two angels to differ as individual members of the same species, even though they are incorporeal substances.

Bonaventure did not deny that angels may differ in the way that species differ, as well as in the way that individuals differ. Nor did he deny that angels are ranked in an ascending series from lowest to highest. However, the gradation of inferior and superior angels may represent differences in degree, which are like individual differences, not differences in kind, which are like specific differences.

The two possible answers to the question about how angels are differentiated and ordered are like undecidable propositions in a mathematical system. On the basis of the limited set of premises from which we started, we cannot decide between them on philosophical grounds. Nor, for that matter, are there any crucial passages in Sacred Scriptures that can be used to adjudicate the dispute between the two great mediaeval theologians.

(4) Angelic Occupation of Space and Movement Through It

Our conception of angels as incorporeal substances precludes us from asking a categorical question about their occupation of physical space or their movement through it.

However, a hypothetical question can be asked, though it must be confessed at once that the thought of it might not occur were it not for religious beliefs concerning the action of angels in relation to human beings and the human environment. Be that as it may, the supposition that angels act on bodies in the physical world does not put us outside the bounds of possibility.

Making the required suppositions, let us then ask: If angels really exist and if some angels act on or in relation to bodies, does that involve them in the occupation of physical space or in movement through it?

Being incorporeal, angels obviously cannot act on bodies as one body acts on another by the direct exercise of physical force or by the exertion of physical influence through an intervening physical medium.

Newton posited the ether as the medium needed for the propagation of light waves and of gravitational attraction. Later theories of light dispensed with the ether. With respect to the attraction exerted by one body upon another at a distance, the gravitational field replaced it.

However, as spiritual beings, angels can exert spiritual power. Can spiritual power be exerted in a way that affects bodies or produces physical effects?

To answer that question, let us consider two phenomena with which we are acquainted. Corporations are not bodies. Legally, they are regarded as "moral persons," entities that can be held responsible for their actions. If they disobey laws, they can be prosecuted; they can be sued for negligence and so on.

Corporations have the power to act on bodies and on the physical environment. They can act at a distance, exerting their influence without the intervention of a physical medium. It also makes sense to say that a corporation is present—spiritually, not physically—at whatever place it acts, and that its presence through the power it exerts at that given place excludes other corporations from acting there at the same time.

The other phenomenon that has relevance to the subject under consideration is in the sphere of what has been called "parapsychology." Some human beings claim to have the power of "telekinesis"—a word that has been coined to designate the psychological, not physical, power of acting on bodies without touching them or exerting any physical influence through an intervening physical medium.

Let us waive for the moment any question about the genuineness of the demonstrations of telekinesis that have been offered. We can still look upon telekinesis as an illustration of what is meant when we speak of angelic action on bodies as the exertion of a psychic or spiritual power.

If angels act spiritually on bodies, the following things can be said about such action.

First, an angel is spiritually present at whatever place in physical space happens to be occupied by the body on which it acts. It can be present at that place without leaving Heaven, which is its spiritual residence, just as a corporation that has its legal residence in Delaware can act in Honolulu without leaving the state in which it is incorporated.

Second, being spiritually present at the place occupied by the body on which it acts, it cannot be present at any other physical place at the same time. In this respect, curiously enough, angels are more like bodies than they are like corporations.

A body cannot be at two places at the same time, but a corporation can exert its influence in many directions and so be spiritually present at many places at the same time. The theologians tell us that God, being an infinite spirit, can be present by His power everywhere at once. In contrast, an angel, being a finite spirit, is more circumscribed in its spiritual action. Acting at one place, it cannot act at another at the same time. It would appear, then, that legally constituted corporations are more like God than they are like angels, but with this qualification added, namely, that unlike God, no corporation can act everywhere at once.

Third, when an angel acts spiritually on a particular body, its presence at the place occupied by that body is also an occupation of that place. The body occupies that particular place *extensively* by filling it with its bulk. In contrast, the angel occupies that place *intensively* by surrounding it with its power. The body is enveloped by the place it occupies. In contrast, the place is enveloped by the angel that is present there by its power.

It follows, therefore, that two angels cannot occupy the same place at the same time. The intensive occupation of a place by spiritual power is as exclusive as the extensive occupation of a place by physical bulk. Just as the physical presence of one body at a place excludes all others from occupying that place, so the spiritual presence of an angel at a place excludes all others from occupying that place. One angel intensively occupying the head of a pin excludes all others from being spiritually present there.

In short, if it ever entered the mind of a frivolous angel to dance on the head of a pin, its whimsical impulse would have to be exercised in a solitary fashion. It could not invite other angels to join it. It would have to dance there alone.

Let us turn now from angelic occupation of space to angelic movement in or through space. Can an angel move from one place to another? Yes, but not in the same way that a body moves from one place to another. When a body moves, its bulk is shifted from this place to that. When an angel moves, its spiritual power shifts from this place to that. The difference between angelic movement from place to place and the local motion of bodies corresponds to the difference between the angelic and the bodily occupation of place.

When an angel moves from place to place by exerting its spiritual power first at one place and then at another, does it move through or traverse the intervening points in space that lie between the places occupied by the two bodies thus acted on?

This leads us to another and closely related question. When an angel moves from place to place, does its movement involve a measurable span of time or is it instantaneous—having no duration, taking no time at all?

Until the advent of modern atomic theory, it was generally held that the local motion of bodies is continuous in both space and time. A body does not move from one place to another without passing through all the points of space that intervene between the place from which it moves and the place to which it moves. Nor does a body move from one place to another instantaneously—without taking time to do so, without the duration of a measurable span of time in which its motion occurs.

In the early years of this century, the great Danish physicist, Niels Bohr, developed a theory of the inner workings of an atom that ascribed to electrons within the atom the power of passing from an outer to an inner orbit instantaneously and without traversing the space between the two orbits.

I remember the occasion of a luncheon conversation at the Faculty Club at the University of Chicago in the early twenties when I was the only philosopher at the table, along with a number of eminent physicists, two of them Nobel laureates. One of them commented on the novelties involved in the Bohr model of what goes on inside an atom.

To the astonishment and, I should add, the discomfort of the physicists at the table, I remarked that the novelty of the two things Niels Bohr said about the jumping of electrons from one orbit to another had been anticipated in mediaeval angelology by similar statements about the local motion of angels.

In their local motion, angels sometimes move like the massive bodies in Isaac Newton's celestial mechanics—going from place to place by passing through all the points in the intervening space and requiring a span of time to do so. But they also sometimes move like the electrons in Niels Bohr's early version of quantum mechanics—transferring the exertion of their spiritual power over a body in one place to a body in another by doing so instantaneously and without passing through all the points in the space between the two bodies.

We noted earlier that if angels really exist, they are neither like bodies, temporal beings, nor like God, eternal. As finite spiritual beings, they exist in a manner that lies between temporality and eternity: their existence is aeviternal.

The theologians tell us that when angelic motion from place to place is not instantaneous, the duration of the motion is not a measurable span of physical time. So, too, when the local motion of an angel is continuous rather than discontinuous, the translation of its spiritual power from one place to another is not the same as the passage of a body through the space that intervenes between one place and another.

(5) *Angels as Knowers*

The definition of an angel, which is the first of our initial premises, states that an angel is not only an incorporeal substance, not only a spiritual being, but also a mind without a body and one that is not associated with a body that is its own.

When we speak of the human mind, our use of the word "mind" comprehends in its connotation not only the intellectual powers of understanding, judging, and reasoning, but also the sensitive powers of perceiving, remembering, and imagining. Whatever view is held concerning the relation between the exercise of the human mind's intellectual powers and the action of the central nervous system and brain, it is generally thought that the mind's sensitive powers cannot be exercised without the involvement of the sense organs and the brain.

To conceive of an angel as a mind without a body and unassociated with a body necessarily entails the deprivation of any and all sensitive powers when we come to consider the action of the angelic mind.

The angelic mind is purely intellectual. It is nothing but an intellect and, as we will presently see, as an intellect, it is nothing but a power of understanding.

Unlike the human intellect, whose powers include that of judging and of reasoning, the angelic intellect does not think. It neither joins nor disjoins concepts to form judgments, as the human mind does; nor does it put judgments together in a process of reasoning that leads to a conclusion. In short, its action is neither cogitative nor discursive. It is purely intuitive. Why this is so remains to be seen.

There is another and more obvious difference between the human mind and the angelic intellect—the one a mind that is closely associated with a body of its own; the other a mind without a body. As noted earlier, the human mind has both sensitive and intellectual powers. It must now be added that the human mind exercises these disparate powers cooperatively and interactively. In forming ideas or concepts, the human mind draws upon its sense-perceptions, memories, and imaginations.

Human beings learn what they know from sense-experience initially, though they may go beyond all sense-experience in the flights of their imagination and in the reach of their thought to the consideration of objects for which no perceptible examples can ever be found.

Even so, we recognize the chasm between the purely imaginary and the real by reference to sense-experience; and we test, also by reference to sense-experience, the validity of our thinking about any objects for which we claim that they have real existence in addition to their being objects of thought.

When we describe the human processes of judging, cogitating, or reasoning, as discursive, our use of the word "discursive" carries with it the connotation of taking time. Only the simple intellectual act of understanding—of apprehending an object of thought—is instantaneous. The same can be said of the simple sensitive act of apprehending a perceptual object.

Both of these acts can be called intuitive rather than discursive because they are instantaneous rather than involving a span of time.

Please note that I am here using the word "intuitive" in a way that differs from its familiar colloquial use to describe the experience of a thought jumping into our minds without our being able to give any explanation of how we came to have it. That colloquial use of the word "intuition" refers to an unpremeditated insight that just happens to turn out to be true. The strict use of the word "intuition" refers to immediate knowledge that has certitude.

From our conception of the angel as a purely spiritual substance and, therefore, as a purely intellectual being—a mind without a body—it follows that the action of the angelic intellect must differ from the action of the human mind in all the respects so far indicated.

Since an angel cannot form ideas from sense-experience, how does it get the ideas by which it knows and understands intuitively (not rationally or discursively) what it does know and understand?

This is a categorical, not a hypothetical question. We do not need to begin by saying "If an angel knows or understands anything," because a purely intellectual being that did not know or understand anything would be null and void.

We can, of course, ask the following hypothetical question: "If angels really exist, does their real existence necessarily involve their knowing and understanding?" The answer to that question is categorically affirmative. It would be impossible for a pure intellect to be actual without its actuality involving the act of knowing and understanding.

From this it also necessarily follows that, if angels really exist, they cannot ever cease from the act of knowing and understanding. Their actuality is inseparable from such action. Unlike the human mind, the angelic mind never goes to sleep.

Let us now return to the question that remains unanswered. How does an angel acquire the ideas by which it intuitively knows and understands whatever it knows and understands? The only conceivable answer is that the ideas involved in angelic knowledge and understanding must be innate or connatural.

On the supposition that the angels are created by God (a supposition the philosopher can make as an entertainable possibility), the answer just given can be expanded.

Just as we, according to the *Declaration of Independence*, are endowed by our creator with certain unalienable rights, so the angels are endowed by their creator with certain infused ideas. The innate ideas that are connatural to them constitute the natures they have as creatures of God.

In creating a multitude of angels, God diversified their several natures by implanting different sets of ideas in each. We can now understand a little better a point that was made earlier, namely, that no two angels are equal in their natures.

Each is higher or lower in rank than another by virtue of the set of infused ideas by which it understands and knows. The higher angels understand more by means of fewer, but more universal or comprehensive, ideas. The lower angels understand less by means of a greater number of ideas that are less universal or comprehensive.

This differentiation of angelic natures from one another would appear to involve essential, not accidental, differences. An angel is what it is by virtue of the ideas it has. If so, this favors the view that one angel differs from another as one species of substance differs from another rather than as one individual differs from another within a single species. It must be remembered, of course, that the notion of species here employed is the philosophical conception of species as ordered in the way that the whole numbers or the regular polygons are ordered.

Since the ideas by which angels intuitively know and understand come from God, the angelic intellect is as infallible as the

Divine intellect. However, the difference between the infinite being of God and the finite being of angels carries with it the acknowledgment that the angelic intellect may be infallible but that, unlike the Divine intellect, it is not omniscient.

A number of other consequences follow from what has already been said. Angels are able to know and understand God better than the human intellect can, precisely because such knowledge and understanding comes to them by way of ideas infused in them by God, not reached by arduous reflection and reasoning with concepts drawn from sense-experience or notions otherwise constructed.

Angels also know themselves better than human beings do because their self-knowledge is purely or entirely reflexive. For a human being to know himself or herself, the human mind must consider the human being as a whole—a corporeal substance, a body having a mind. The human being as a whole is not a purely intelligible object. That is precisely what an angel is, being a purely intellectual being. An angel is, therefore, able to understand itself much more directly and completely than a human being can.

The ideas by which an angel knows itself are such that they enable an angel to know not only all lower angels, but also everything that all lower angels know. It also can know higher angels, but not everything that higher angels know.

Angelic knowledge and understanding extends to the physical cosmos—the world of corporeal things. The inferior and limited human intellect is able to know such things by sense-experience, reflection, and reasoning. A fortiori, angels are able to know and understand such things better by knowing them intuitively by means of the innate ideas God implanted in their created natures.

The human mind can know singulars—this or that individual thing—only by sense-perception, not conceptually or by an act of understanding. An angel, on the contrary, can know and understand this or that individual corporeal substance by means of its infused ideas.

Being finite and, therefore, not omniscient, the angelic intellect is subject to certain limitations. Here, the philosopher must turn to the theologian to learn what knowledge belongs only to God because of Divine omniscience.

In addition to God's knowledge of himself, in which angels can participate only supernaturally through grace and not naturally by their own innate ideas, Divine knowledge includes two things that are beyond the natural knowledge of angels. One is what will happen in the temporal future of the physical cosmos. The other is what goes on in the hearts and minds of human beings.

(6) *Angels as Lovers*

When we consider the human mind, we distinguish between (a) its cognitive and (b) its appetitive powers; that is, (a) its powers of knowing, by sense or intellect or both; and (b) its powers of desiring, by the passions of the body that are associated with the senses or by the will that is associated with the intellect.

Since angels are purely spiritual beings, they cannot have any passions or bodily desires. As spiritual beings, it is possible for them to have a will as well as an intellect. If so, they can not only know the good, but also will it.

If we attribute free choice to the human will in relation to good and evil, we should, *a fortiori*, attribute free choice to the angelic will. However, it is necessary to remember the theological doctrine that the angelic exercise of free choice, by which the good angels were separated from the demons, occurred only once at the beginning of time.

The willing of the good, divorced from all acquisitive desire, is one of the meanings of the word "love." In the realm of human affairs, that powerful word has many meanings. We sometimes use it to refer to sexual desire. We sometimes extend its meaning to include more than sexual desire by adding the component of genuine affection for the sexual partner, in which case we may elevate it above mere sexuality by calling it "erotic love."

It is also possible for love to occur in complete separation from

sex. It can exist in a world without sex. Such is the love that is
the highest form of friendship in which no sensual pleasure is
involved and no useful purpose served. The beloved is simply
loved or admired for his or her own sake, for the goodness he
or she exhibits. Such love is completely benevolent rather than
acquisitive. It consists not only in admiring the goodness of the
object loved, but also in willing its good.

When human beings love God, or themselves, or their neighbors as themselves, the love in each case is purely an act of will
on their part, involving no ingredients of bodily passion or acquisitive desire. That love, the theologians tell us, may be natural or it may be the supernatural love that the theologians call
charity, which human beings enjoy only as a gift of God's grace.

The theological addenda having been noted, we can proceed
philosophically by asking the following questions.

The first is a categorical question: Does our conception of the
angelic nature justify our attributing a will as well as an intellect to angels? Man's having a will as well as an intellect does
not depend upon his having a body. Such dependence applies
only to human emotions or passions, all of which involve corporeal organs. Since man's having a will does not depend upon
his having a body, the lack of a body does not preclude an angel's having a will as well as an intellect.

The good is either an object of acquisitive desire or an object
of admiration and benevolent love. When an object is understood to be good, it also becomes an object of desire or love.
Angelic knowledge includes an understanding of the goodness of
the objects known—the goodness of God, the goodness of themselves, and the goodness of other angels.

Angels cannot have acquisitive desires, for there is no way in
which they can improve or perfect themselves by acquiring external goods. Understanding the goodness of the objects they
know must, therefore, be associated with an act of will by which
they admire and love those objects for the goodness inherent in
them.

Hence, we must give an affirmative answer to the following

hypothetical question: "If angels really exist, do they love God, first of all, and then themselves and other angels, all objects they know by the ideas infused in their natures by God; all objects the intrinsic goodness of which they also understand?" The angelic love just affirmed is both natural and an act of free choice.

Here the theologians add that the good angels, and only the good angels, may also enjoy supernatural love—the charity that God bestows as a gift of grace. It is the deprivation of this gift that constitutes the everlasting damnation of Satan and the demons associated with him in his fall—a deprivation that, as we noted earlier, resulted from their rejection of God's gift by a free choice on their part.

(7) *The Community and Communication of Angels*

Human society includes men of goodwill and men who are otherwise motivated. The association of human beings in political communities or civil societies is accompanied by some measure of peace only to the extent that their life together and their interaction are governed by just laws. Such government must include the exercise of the coercive force needed to gain obedience to law from those who do not obey laws simply by recognizing the authority that their justice confers upon them.

Civil peace seldom, if ever, prevails flawlessly. It is not only flawed by criminal breaches of the peace; it is also defective by reason of imperfect or inefficient government and unjust or unenforced laws.

In our philosophical consideration of a society of angels, we must proceed without any acknowledgment of the division of angels into the good who enjoy life in Heaven and the evil who are damned in Hell. That division belongs to theological, not philosophical, discourse about angels.

The community of angels with which we are concerned is the heavenly host—the company of those angels who by their knowledge and will, their choice and love, live in grace and glory, enjoying the presence of God.

The philosopher cannot affirm that such a heavenly community exists. Yet, there is nothing impossible about it. Hence, he can ask the hypothetical question, "If it does really exist, what is it like as compared with human society on earth?"

Two answers immediately spring to mind. In the first place, it is a society of perfect concord and flawless peace. In this respect, it is remarkably different from our earthly cities or states. In the second place, it is a society in which the Divine law that governs it—the two precepts of charity—need not be accompanied by coercive force. Angelic obedience to the precepts of Divine law is an indefectible response, flowing naturally from the goodness of the angelic will, and also supernaturally from the charity that is a gift of God's grace.

In the hypothetical society of angels thus envisioned, do the angels communicate with one another? If so, in what manner? A philosopher can ask this question, but he cannot answer it. Nothing in his initial premises, however extended their implications, provides him with a basis for answering it.

However, the theologian does offer answers to it, either on the solid basis of scriptural passages or on the questionable authority of Dionysius. Aquinas, for example, tells us, first, that higher angels enlighten lower angels; inferior angels cannot enlighten superior angels in any way. Aquinas tells us, second, that in the society of angels, one angel cannot move the will of another.

The theologian's third contribution concerns the speech of angels. Here, the theologian distinguishes between physical and telepathic communication, regarding both as forms of speech.

Communication is physical speech if it must employ physical sounds, signs, or gestures to convey thoughts or wishes from one person to another. It is telepathic speech if the conveyance of thoughts or wishes is accomplished without the employment of any physical medium of communication.

The enlightenment of lower angels by higher angels is the result of telepathic speech by the higher to the lower angels. However, the theologian then points out that while every instance of angelic enlightenment involves angelic speech, the reverse is not the case.

Angelic speech can occur without angelic enlightenment and, so, lower angels can communicate telepathically with higher angels, even though they cannot enlighten them. What the lower angels communicate to the higher angels is not what they know or understand, but only what they wish or desire—what they tend toward by their wills.

According to the theologian, angels speak to God, but only in the sense that they communicate the receptivity of their will to God's grace and the obedience of their will to God's law.

Two more questions remain for the theologian to answer. Is there some measure of privacy in the telepathic communication of one angel with another, or is angelic speech overheard by all? This the theologian answers without reference to scriptural passages or any other authority. He simply points out that one human being can speak to another alone and in complete privacy, adding "much more so can this be the case among angels."

The last question asks whether distance is an impediment to angelic communication. It should be obvious, at once, that it cannot be. Distance may impede the effectiveness of communication by physical speech, or even prevent it, but angelic speech, because it is telepathic, suffers no such impediment.

The question itself should never have been raised. Since heaven is not a physical place, the members of the angelic society who communicate with one another there are not separated from one another by spatial distances.

PART FOUR

Angelistic Fallacies in Modern Thought

9

How Like an Angel!

(1) *And How Unlike!*

IN ACT II, Scene ii, of the play, Shakespeare's Hamlet delivers an eloquent and memorable eulogy of mankind.

What a piece of work is a man! how noble in reason! how infinite in faculty, in form and moving! how express and admirable in action! in apprehension how like an angel! how like a god! the beauty of the world! the paragon of animals!

And, changing his tone of voice, Hamlet then adds: "And yet to me, what is this quintessence of dust?"

Another deliverance on the subject comes to us from Blaise Pascal, who takes up where Hamlet leaves off:

What a chimera, then, is man! What a novelty! What a monster, what a chaos, what a contradiction, what a prodigy! Judge of all things, imbecile, worm of the earth; depository of truth, a sink of uncertainty and error; the pride and refuse of the universe.

Continuing on the same subject, Pascal adds: "Man is neither angel nor brute, and the unfortunate thing is that he who would act the angel acts the brute."

I know that quarreling, on philosophical grounds, with the accuracy of a poet's words is not the thing to do. But the words are, after all, Hamlet's, and Hamlet is delivering a somewhat ironical oration on the subject. My objection is summed up in

Pascal's statement: "Man is neither angel nor brute." Hamlet's "how like an angel" needs to be supplemented by the immediate addition of "and also how unlike an angel."

In our philosophical consideration of angels, just completed, readers will have noted and remembered that, at every point, it was necessary to preface what could be said about angelic attributes and actions by first describing the human condition as a basis of comparison and contrast. At every turn, it was the differences, not the likenesses, that helped to underline a point of critical importance to our understanding of angelic being, knowing, and action.

All of these crucial differences stem from a single radical difference between the angels and us—our corporeality, their incorporeality.

We have minds that are inseparable in their operation from the action of our bodies, intellects dependent on our perceptions, memories, and imaginations, wills affected by the turbulence and driving impulses of our passions.

We have a temporal existence, coming into being with the bodily trauma of birth and perishing with the terminal trauma of death.

We are finite individuals, with a limited duration in time and a limited location in terrestrial space.

We are subject to every variety of change and to all the vicissitudes of outrageous fortune. We go through a life cycle of growth and decline; we improve or deteriorate; we learn and forget; we lose consciousness; we go to sleep.

In all this inventory of characteristics, only one thing can be said univocally of the angels and us. They and we are both finite beings. They and we need not exist—are capable of not existing. They and we are not eternal.

In all other respects, they differ from us. Anything else that we can say affirmatively about both the angels and us must be said analogically, not univocally. Every indication of a likeness between them and us—with regard to their and our knowing or understanding, their and our loving, their and our willing or acting—must be immediately qualified by the radical difference between them and us.

(2) *The Two Extremes*

In the realm of possibility, we conceive angels as purely spiritual beings. In the realm of actuality, we think of ourselves in one of three ways: (i) as purely corporeal or material beings; (ii) as a conjunction or association of two quite separate substances, one a body and the other a spirit—a rational soul or mind; or (iii) as beings having both a material and a spiritual aspect, admixed or fused in such a way that the aspects are inseparable.

Two of these three ways that have emerged in the history of Western thought are, in my judgment, erroneous—the first and the second. They are not erroneous to the same extent or for the same reason.

All three of the ways in which man has conceived himself made their initial appearance in antiquity. The earliest was the purely materialistic view of man developed by the Greek atomist, Democritus and his Roman disciple, Epicurus—a theory celebrated in the great philosophical poem by Lucretius *On the Nature of Things*. According to the completely materialistic doctrine of the ancient atomists, man is made up of nothing but atoms and the void, or the empty spaces in which the atoms ceaselessly move about. There is nothing of soul or spirit in the composition of human nature. Man is nothing but a composite body, constituted by material units of one sort or another. The immortality of the human soul or spirit, which Plato so unhesitatingly affirmed on his view of the soul as not needing a body to exist, the materialists as readily and emphatically deny.

The materialistic view was followed by a conception of man that went almost to the opposite extreme, the Platonic conception of man as a union of two quite distinct substances—a body and a rational soul or intellect, the latter capable of a separate existence and also capable of transmigrating from one body to another.

The third view, advanced by Aristotle, attempted to correct what he thought to be the errors in the two extreme views. In his conception of human nature, man is neither just a body or a collocation of atoms nor a union of two quite distinct and separable substances, one material and the other spiritual—one a body and the other a rational soul or mind.

In Aristotle's view, man is a single substance and, in that respect, is like every other individual thing in the physical cosmos. However, unlike every other corporeal substance, man, as a single substance, is composite of matter and spirit, of material and immaterial aspects—the immaterial aspect consisting in the intellectual power that distinguishes man from other animals.

According to this third view, man is neither entirely a material thing, composed of elementary particles of matter or quanta of energy, nor is he compounded of two substances as alien to one another as body and soul or matter and mind. He is a living organism like any other animal, but he is distinguished from all other animals by virtue of having a mind or intellect—the powers and operations of which cannot be explained by the action of the brain.

Brain action is a necessary, but not a sufficient, condition for the occurrence of mental operations or processes. There is, in short, something immaterial about man, something spiritual in the sense that it is not reducible to bodily parts or movements and not explicable entirely by reference to them.

What has been said earlier in this chapter about all the differences between angels and us indicates that I look upon the Aristotelian conception of human nature as the correct view of it. My judgment that the Platonic view is erroneous can best be expressed by saying that it is ridden with angelistic fallacies. An angelistic fallacy consists in attributing to man attributes or powers that belong only to purely spiritual substances—to minds without bodies and not associated with bodies that are somehow their own.

Though, in my judgment, the materialistic view of man is also erroneous, it is not erroneous in the same way or for the same reason. Its only angelistic fallacy, if it can be so called, consists in denying that angels are possible beings. Its denial that angels actually exist is simply a corollary of its denial that anything exists except corporeal substances—bodies in motion.

This fundamental premise of materialism, as we have seen, is not self-evident nor has it ever been demonstrated beyond a reasonable doubt by the marshalling of empirical evidence or by cogent and irrefutable arguments.

On the contrary, it can be put in doubt by evidence inconsistent with it and by arguments that challenge it. What is erroneous about materialism is the dogmatic assertion of the truth of a proposition that is, at best, a questionable assumption.

Of these three views of man, two persisted throughout the Middle Ages—the Platonic and the Aristotelian views. The materialistic view, so repugnant to the religious beliefs that then prevailed, had little or no currency. The Platonic view, at the opposite extreme, was dominant in many circles and during most of the period, precisely because the prevalent religious views found it a support or, at least, no threat. Mediaeval philosophers and theologians who adopted the Platonic view were influenced by the Platonists of the Hellenistic period of the Roman Empire, notably Proclus and Plotinus.

Only toward the end of the Middle Ages did some Jewish, Muslim, and Christian theologians risk their necks by adopting the Aristotelian view as the corrective for the errors of both materialism and Platonism. The risk they took of being charged with heresy arose from what, at first glance, appeared to be threatening challenges to religious belief implicit in the Aristotelian view, especially the article of faith concerning the immortality of the human soul.

In the modern world, the two extreme views reappeared. Hobbes and La Mettrie revived the mechanistic materialism of the ancient atomists that had remained dormant during the Middle Ages. Of the atomistic theories, some took the extreme form of denying soul or spirit entirely and reducing mind to matter; some, the more moderate form of recognizing an analytical distinction between mental and material events, still insisting that the action of the brain is not only a necessary but also a sufficient condition for all mental processes.

Descartes and Leibnitz gave new life to the Platonism that persisted throughout the Middle Ages. More than that, they explicitly espoused the angelistic fallacies entailed by the Platonic conception of man.

The Platonic view is still current today, surprisingly even among Catholic philosophers who insist that Aquinas is more Platonic than he is usually supposed to be. While engaged in writing this book, I ran across an article, entitled "Man an Embodied Spirit," in a Catholic philosophical journal. The writer contended that the Thomistic conception of man is that of an incarnate spirit, and went on to say that "a human being is not so much the highest of the animals—a rational animal—but the lowest of the angels, an enfleshed spirit."

The main lines in the development of philosophical thought in the modern world are determined by the dogmatic materialism of Hobbes, by the angelistic fallacies of the Platonism adopted by Descartes and Leibnitz, by the persistence of both extremes in later centuries, sometimes attenuated and sometimes exaggerated in their reaction against one another, and, finally, by the effort to avoid all the controversies that had arisen by turning philosophy entirely in another direction, one in which, it should be added, no clear view of man has emerged.

None of these modern thinkers appears to have been sufficiently cognizant or sufficiently appreciative of the Aristotelian corrective of the two extreme views that had finally become regnant at the end of the Middle Ages. One cannot name a single eminent philosopher from the sixteenth to the nineteenth century who adopted the Aristotelian view and used it to challenge dogmatic materialism, on the one end, or to correct the angelistic fallacies of modern Platonism, on the other hand.

That is why in dealing with these angelistic fallacies, I have stressed their influence on modern thought. They were detected and corrected by Aristotle in antiquity and by Aristotelians at the end of the Middle Ages. Their work was for the most part ignored or forgotten, and so the conception of man that lies between the two extremes does not play its part in modern thought.

The foregoing statement needs one addendum. In the twentieth century, the French Roman Catholic philosopher Jacques Maritain, himself an Aristotelian and a Thomist, did his best to reinstate the Aristotelian middle view by calling attention to the angelistic fallacies that are so pronounced in the philosophy of Descartes. His book, *Three Reformers*, contains an essay entitled "Descartes, or the Incarnation of the Angel."

In it, Maritain not only laid bare all the angelistic fallacies in Cartesian philosophy, but also traced their consequences in modern thought down to Kant and Hegel and beyond.

Little errors in the beginning, Aristotle said long ago, have serious consequences in the end. The angelistic fallacies are hardly little errors, and they have had very serious consequences, indeed.

Maritain's essay was, however, ignored by thinkers outside the narrow circle of scholastic philosophy in which he moved. I offer what follows as a much briefer and, perhaps, a more readable account of the telling points that Maritain made in that essay.

(3) *The Incarnation of the Angel*

We are here concerned mainly with angelistic fallacies concerning the human mind or, more precisely, with the human intellect as a power of knowing and understanding distinct from the sensitive powers of perception, memory, and imagination. Making that distinction clear and sharp is, by the way, a tenet shared by Platonists and Aristotelians, but not by materialists.

Let me begin by repeating something said earlier about the Cartesian view of man. According to Descartes, man is a composite of two distinct substances—one an intellect, which he called *res cogitans* or, in English, a thinking substance; the other a body, which he called *res extensa* or, in English, a three-dimensionally extended substance.

The definition of an angel as a possible mode of being includes the notion of the angel as an intellect—a *res cogitans*. Unlike the intellect that enters into the composition of man, according to Descartes, the angelic intellect is not associated with a body that is its own. Otherwise, the human and the angelic intellect are very much alike in the Cartesian view, though not completely so.

Neither is in any way dependent upon a body for the exercise of its powers; neither requires recourse to sense-perception, sensory memory, or acts of imagination for its attainment of the knowledge and understanding that is its proper possession.

The human incarnation of an intellect that is angelic in character does not consist in its embodiment in a way that requires cooperation between the intellect and the sensitive faculties in the process of knowing; nor, for that matter, does it involve the influence of bodily passions on the will in the volitional sphere.

The association of the human intellect, as an angel incarnate, with a physical body that it does not need for its action, can only be described as a philosophical embarrassment—a mystery that Descartes did not explain, and that nobody can.

Bishop Berkeley's idealism is more extreme than that of Plato or Descartes. His conception of man as a purely spiritual being, which he adopted in consequence of his antimaterialistic denial of the existence of all bodies, human or otherwise, may be as erroneous as the materialistic denial of the existence of anything spiritual.

Whether erroneous or not, neither extreme is plagued by the embarrassment that attends the Cartesian conjunction of an angelic intellect with a human body. They may be caught in other philosophical embarrassments, as they most certainly are, but not in this one.

The angelistic fallacies inherent in the Cartesian view of the human intellect, as an angel incarnate, consist of a number of closely related errors about how the human intellect works.

(1) According to Descartes, the human intellect does not acquire its ideas by reflection upon, and abstraction from, sense-experience with the aid of memory and imagination. That being so, it must be endowed with innate ideas, as angels are.

The doctrine of recollection set forth by Socrates in an early Platonic dialogue, the *Meno*, introduces the theory that men are born with innate ideas. Learning, as Socrates tries to demonstrate in his conversation with the slave-boy, is nothing but a vivification of the ideas innately present in the human mind at birth. Learning consists in their being recollected and brought to life.

To complete the story of this strange doctrine of innate ideas (an angelistic fallacy, if there ever was one), it should be mentioned that in the first book of his *Essay Concerning Human Understanding*, John Locke presented a vigorous refutation of it. That did not put an end to this angelistic fallacy.

It took still another form in Kant's theory of the transcendental categories of the human understanding. They are not derived in any way from sense-experience. Instead, the categories of the understanding, along with the transcendental forms of sensory apprehension, are constitutive of all the experience we have or can possibly have. Both the transcendental categories and the transcendental forms are inherent in the very structure of the human mind. In no other way can certitude be attained.

(2) According to Descartes, when man's angelic intellect operates with its clear and distinct innate ideas, it operates infallibly. When men fall into error, that is due to their wills, not their intellects. Error is voluntary, not intellectual.

Descartes explains human error in the same way that theologians try to explain the mistake made by the infallible intellect of Satan, the highest of all angels. Satan's error must be attributed to his will, not his intellect.

(3) According to Descartes, the proper operation of man's an-

gelic intellect is intuitive, not ratiocinative or discursive. The making of judgments and the drawing of conclusions in a process of reasoning is not properly an intellectual act. Once again, it is the action of the will that Descartes thinks must be involved in anything that goes beyond simple and immediate intellectual intuition.

That being so, Descartes should not have called the intellect a *res cogitans*, or thinking substance, for the human intellect, as such—as left to itself—does not cogitate any more than an angel's does. Maritain aptly described Descartes as a rationalist who disowned reason. This is one of the consequences of his conceiving the human intellect as an angel incarnate.

(4) According to Descartes, the intuitive knowledge or understanding possessed by man's angelic intellect, in virtue of its innate ideas, is possessed by man independently of his having any acquaintance with really existent things.

The angelistic fallacy just mentioned is a curious one, because it involved Descartes in the serious error of making ideas the objects of human knowledge and understanding. Our account of angelic knowledge and understanding treated the ideas implanted in the angelic intellect by God as the *means by which* angels know and understand, not *the objects which* they know and understand. The innate ideas possessed by angels enable them to know and understand real existence—God, themselves, other angels, and the things of this corporeal cosmos.

What is paradoxical about this angelistic fallacy lies in a compounding of errors. On the one hand, it is truly an angelistic fallacy in that it makes man's knowledge independent of acquaintance with the world through sense-experience. Angelic knowledge and understanding is similarly independent.

On the other hand, the fallacy can also be described as falsely angelistic because of Descartes' additional error regarding ideas, whether in the angelic or the human intellect, as *that which* is known or understood rather than as *that by which* reality is known or understood.

This additional error is one of those very little errors in the beginning that have the most serious consequences in the end. It is repeated by Locke, even though Locke disagrees with Descartes about innate ideas.

This error generated all the psychological and epistemological puzzles that have beset modern thought ever after.

It also led to all the mistakes made by philosophers from Hume and Kant onward in their effort to circumvent these puzzles when, instead, they should have eliminated the puzzlements entirely by recognizing that they stemmed from the crucial error made by Descartes and Locke.

The puzzles referred to include the vexatious question about how we can have any knowledge of the external world or even that it exists; the equally vexatious question about how we can get beyond the ideas that are objects of our knowledge and understanding or how our ideas can be both objects of knowledge and also representations of reality.

Included also are a variety of linguistic puzzles, such as how the words we use in talking to one another can enable us to communicate about public objects rather than about the private objects that are the ideas in our separate minds.

The puzzles referred to above and other puzzles, such as the mind-body problem that has been given so much attention in modern thought, are dismissed as pseudoproblems by contemporary philosophers, especially positivists and those who call themselves analysts. That designation of the problems is correct, although the analysts who so designate them do not do so for the right reason. They are pseudoproblems, not genuine problems, because they need not have arisen in the first place.

Regarding them as genuine problems and trying to circumvent them, as Kant and others after him tried to do, is not the right way of handling the matter. Nor is the right way to dismiss them as pseudoproblems without putting a finger on the errors that generated them—errors made by Descartes, Leibnitz, and Locke at the beginning of modern thought.

(5) According to Descartes, man's angelic intellect is always active. It never blacks out and becomes unconscious. It never grows weary or goes to sleep.

Angels never sleep. They are chronic insomniacs. The human intellect, being angelic, is also exempt from fatigue and sleep, however strange that may seem to readers of this book who may have been put to sleep by it.

(6) According to Descartes, man's angelic intellect, operating infallibly with the clear and distinct ideas that are its innate endowment, attains the knowledge it possesses with certitude—beyond the shadow of a doubt. Such knowledge was what Descartes set out to find when he pursued his policy of doubting everything that his predecessors claimed to know.

Angelic knowledge has the certitude that Descartes sought to attain. Where could Descartes find anything like it on earth? Only in mathematics. Why only there? Because the objects of mathematics are ideal objects to know—clear and distinct ideas.

(7) The final consequence of all these angelistic errors is the Cartesian presumption that an individual mind, such as his own, can dispense with any consideration of truths that might be found and sifted from the errors in the thought of his predecessors.

Superior angels, we have found, can enlighten inferior angels. Though man's intellect is angelic, no human intellect, according to Descartes, can enlighten or acquire enlightenment from any other. Each is a world unto itself. Each begins anew, starting from fresh ground, or else clearing it of the rubbish accumulated from the past.

Here, once again, Descartes compounds errors, combining a truly angelistic fallacy with a falsely angelistic fallacy. The angels have innate ideas, but one angel can enlighten or be enlightened by another. The human intellect has innate ideas, but, in the human realm, teaching and learning seem to be excluded by Descartes.

10

Shades of the Prison House

(1) *The Immortality of the Soul*

IN PLATO'S DIALOGUE *Phaedo*, Socrates engages in conversation with friends who have come to his prison cell in somber anticipation of the twilight hour when he will drink the hemlock. Their conversation turns to the question of the immortality of the soul. The time and place for it seems mordantly appropriate.

It is a long conversation with many twists and turns. By questioning those around him in his usual manner, Socrates develops a number of arguments intended to persuade them that the soul is immortal—that it continues in existence after its separation from the mortal body with which it happens to be united, resuming an existence it had before the union.

The truth that the body is mortal needs no arguments for its support. Birth and death are facts of common experience, as well-attested as the alternation of day and night. If the coming to be and passing away of all corporeal things—their generation and degeneration—calls for any explanation, Socrates thinks it is to be found in the fact that they are all made up of material parts or elements that are separable. Degeneration is decomposition.

The soul would be mortal, too, if it were materially constituted and decomposable. The crux of the various arguments that Socrates advances for its immortality, therefore, lies in two assertions he makes about it. It is immaterial; and it is simple, not composite. It must, therefore, continue to exist after the body perishes.

As evening approaches, the friends of Socrates appear to be persuaded of the truth of the conclusion to which he has tried to lead them. The jailer comes in with the cup of hemlock. Saying farewell and expressing a few last wishes, Socrates drinks it. The poison slowly works its way up his body and he dies. His friends break into tears—expressing grief for what has happened to Socrates or for the loss that they themselves have suffered?

The question is more than ironical. Of course, they have suffered a grievous loss. Their friend has passed away. But what loss has Socrates suffered for them to grieve about? If they were persuaded by his arguments, the Socrates that passed away before their eyes did not die.

If that can be said, then we are compelled to ask: *Who was Socrates?* Was Socrates the union of two separate substances— one a mortal body, the other an immortal spirit? Or was Socrates only one of these two substances—an immortal spirit that just happened to be using this particular snub-nosed body for a short span of time?

Before we consider the further difficulties that these questions raise, let us note that the Socratic argument for the immortality of the soul rests upon an assumption even more gratuitous than the materialistic assumption that nothing exists except bodies.

That proposition, as we have seen, is neither self-evident nor demonstrable. Much less self-evident or demonstrable is the proposition that spirits exist. If any cogent reasoning could be advanced to support the proposition that human spirits exist (i.e., souls, as purely spiritual substances), it would also be available to support the proposition that angels exist. We can find none.

Let me be sure that the reader does not rush ahead to false conclusions. I have not undermined or renounced a position for which I argued earlier, namely, that spiritual substances—angels or souls—*can* exist, that they are genuinely *possible* beings. I have not said anything that makes religious faith in the immortality of the human soul an absurdity, because it affirms an impossibility—the continuing existence of the human spirit after death of the body.

The difficulties we must now face arise from the fact that the two possibilities—the possibility that angels really exist and the possibility that souls really exist as purely spiritual substances—do not stand on the same footing philosophically. The first possibility does not cause us any philosophical embarrassments whatsoever. The second overwhelms us with them.

The reason should be obvious at once. Angels are conceived as purely spiritual substances that are not united with bodies. The Socratic argument applies perfectly to them. Being immaterial and incomposite, angels are immortal.

Souls, on the other hand, are not angels precisely because they are united with bodies. In addition, Socrates contends that their being united with bodies is the source or principle of the life enjoyed by the bodies with which they are united.

The difference between animate and inanimate bodies is identical with the difference between besouled bodies and bodies lacking souls. All living organisms have souls, plants and animals as well as human beings, the only difference being that human souls are rational.

Are plant and animal souls immortal, too? Whether the answer is affirmative or negative, embarrassments arise, both philosophical and theological.

Why are plant and animal souls not immortal, if human souls are? Why are human souls immortal, if plant and animal souls are not? These are difficult questions to answer philosophically. The difficulty is compounded by the fact that only human souls have been declared immortal by the three great Western religions, a point on which they differ from contrary pronouncements by certain Far Eastern religions.

(2) *One or Two?*

Waiving all the difficulties we have so far considered, we are still left with the one most germane to our present concern with angelistic fallacies.

The Platonic view of the human soul—as a spiritual substance somehow united with a human body—and the Cartesian view of the human intellect—as an immaterial thinking substance somehow united with a human body as a material extended substance—are for the most part indistinguishable. I will call attention to one important difference between them later.

On both views, we cannot avoid or bypass the following questions: Is a human being one or two? Is a human being two quite separate things as are a boat and the rower who moves it?

In the latter case, the boat can sink, and the rower survive—if the rower has the ability to swim. So, too, it would appear that the body can die, in fact, must die, when the soul jumps out of it; and the soul can survive, in fact, must survive, if it can persevere in existence when separated from the body.

Only if body and soul are quite separate things or substances, as the boat and the rower are, are they also quite separable, so that one can cease to exist while the other perseveres in existence. But, then, what is a human being? Who is Socrates? The union of the two or just the soul that temporarily inhabits the body and bestows life on it by moving it, as the rower moves the boat?

The classical schoolbook syllogism, "All men are mortal; Socrates is a man; therefore, Socrates is mortal," would appear to answer the question by saying that a man is just one thing, and that Socrates is mortal because he, too, is just one thing, not two. To hold the contrary view—the Platonic and Cartesian view—that a human being is not one but two substances would require us to alter the reasoning in the following manner.

Human beings are partly mortal and partly immortal. They are alive as long as body and soul are united. They are partly mortal because, when the soul leaves the body, the body dies; they are partly immortal because the soul can leave the body without dying. It is not only the source of the body's life, it also has a life of its own.

So far, so good, but who, then, is Socrates? Should that proper name be affixed only to the union of his soul and body or to his soul by itself, when it leaves the body, causing its death and continuing to live?

If we say both are Socrates, the proper name is rendered ambiguous. It refers to two quite different things.

If we say only the union of soul and body is Socrates, we can say that Socrates is mortal, for the soul that continues to live after the death of Socrates is not Socrates.

If we say only the soul is Socrates, we can say that Socrates is immortal, but, then, the person who died by drinking the hemlock was not Socrates.

The Platonic and Cartesian views, both of which conceive the human soul as if it were an angel, cannot avoid the conclusion that Socrates and every human being is two things, not one, with all the philosophical and theological embarrassments that inexorably follow from that conclusion.

On the basis of that conclusion, theologians would be forced to make a serious retraction. They insist that angels and souls are radically different kinds of spiritual substances. They tell us that when the souls of the saved, on leaving the body, go to heaven, they join the company of angels there, but they do not become angels. The angelic host and the communion of saints may form one heavenly community, but it is a heterogeneous, not a homogeneous, society.

The reason why theologians insist that angels and souls are radically different kinds of spiritual substances is that an angel by its nature is not associated with a body that is its very own. Each soul is united with one body and only one, uniquely its own.

That is why Jewish, Christian, and Muslim theologians reject the doctrine of the transmigration of souls—a doctrine cherished by contrary Far Eastern religions and also proposed as a myth in the dialogues of Plato.

Of a different sort are the philosophical embarrassments consequent upon the Platonic and Cartesian view of the human soul as identical in being with an angel—a purely spiritual substance that does not need a body either for its existence or for its proper operation, which is intuitive intellection. Why, then, is it united with a body to form a boat-and-rower combination of two quite disparate and separable things?

That problem is as insoluble as the so-called mind-body problem that goes along with it.

Also insoluble is the problem of what differentiates one soul from another, considered to be independent of the bodies with which they are united.

Angels without bodies, we have seen, are differentiated by the different sets of innate ideas that God implants in their natures at creation. As thus differentiated, it would appear that angels differ specifically from one another, not as individuals do that are members of the same species.

Do Plato and Descartes think that all human souls have the same set of innate ideas, or does each human soul have a set that is distinctively its own? On the first alternative, all human souls would be members of the same species and would have to differ individually from one another, but how? On the second alternative, each soul would differ in species from every other, as angels do, but, then, what becomes of the notion of a single human species?

(3) More Like an Angel

I promised earlier to call attention to one important difference between Descartes and Plato, though both commit the same angelistic fallacy about the rational soul of man.

One was a Christian as well as a philosopher, and the other, a philosopher who was not a Christian. Plato could, therefore, embrace the doctrine—or what was for him the myth—of the transmigration of souls. Descartes could not. That, however, is not the important philosophical difference between them. It consists rather in the difference between Plato's theory of ideas and that of Descartes.

For Plato, the innate ideas in the human mind are not the

objects of human knowledge. They are the psychological instrumentalities human beings employ to attain knowledge. The knowledge, thereby attained, is knowledge of ideas that exist quite independently of the human mind and that constitute the fundamental reality to be known.

Plato distinguishes the realm of being from the realm of becoming. In one are the eternal ideas that have reality in themselves. In the other are the forever changing material things that have reality only to the extent that they participate in the eternal ideas. They are nothing but shadows of reality and, as such, are objects of opinion, not of knowledge.

For Descartes, the opposite is the case. The realm of becoming—the world of ever-changing physical things—is reality for him, though his affirmation of the existence of God and of angels makes reality larger than the realm of becoming. It includes real beings that either do not change or do not change in the way that material substances do.

Here, then, is the crucial difference between Plato and Descartes. For Plato, ideas in the human mind (ideas with a small "i") are the means whereby the human mind or rational soul knows the reality of the eternal Ideas (Ideas with a capital "I"). For Descartes, ideas in the human mind are, themselves, the objects known. Descartes and all who follow him in this error are never able to explain how reality, which should be the knowable, is known.

Plato's conception of man's rational soul makes it a spiritual substance that has an independent existence of the sort that angels are affirmed by religious faith to have and are supposed by philosophical thought to be capable of having.

The same can be said of Descartes' conception of man's intellect as one of the two substances that enter into the composition of a human being. It also regards the human intellect as if it were an angel.

But the rational soul, in Plato's conception, is *more* like an angel than is the human intellect as Descartes conceives it. Like the angels, rational souls, in Plato's theory of the matter, employ their innate ideas to know reality. Unlike the angels, human intellects, according to Descartes, know only their own ideas.

(4) *The Incarceration of the Soul*

William Wordsworth's great poem, "Ode on the Intimations of Immortality," contains the following lines:

> Our birth is but a sleep and a forgetting:
> The soul that rises with us, our life's Star,
>   Hath had elsewhere its setting,
>   And cometh from afar;
>   Not in entire forgetfulness,
>   And not in utter nakedness,
> But trailing clouds of glory do we come
>   from God, who is our home:
> Heaven lies about us in our infancy!
> Shades of the prison house begin to close
>   Upon the growing Boy. . . .

There, we have a magnificently lyrical rendition of a Christianized version of the Platonic doctrine of the human soul, its origin, its immortality, and its relation to the body with which it is united.

One point it makes, and one upon which I wish to dwell for a moment, is also to be found in the Platonic dialogues. *The body is the prison house of the soul.* The soul is not just united with the body. It is imprisoned there. The incarnation of the angel-like being of a human soul is a penal incarceration of it.

When the human soul is thought to have all or most of the properties of an angel, thinking of it as united with a body is not only a disturbing thought because inexplicable. Much worse than that, it is a disturbing thought because it would appear that the soul is being penalized by that incarceration.

The soul, being like an angel, is much better off when it is not associated with or imprisoned in a body. That is a much more appropriate state of being for it to enjoy.

The death of the body frees the soul from these mortal coils. Death is an emancipation for the soul, an end to its imprisonment. Plato says so explicitly in a number of places; similar views are expressed in certain Far Eastern religions.

In one famous passage, Socrates declares that the philosopher's life should be one of dying or, at least, of trying to approximate what death finally achieves—emancipation from the body. He also recommends asceticism as a philosophical way of life. These, too, are precepts—ways of life to be followed—recommended by certain Far Eastern religions, and adopted in Christianity when mortification of the flesh is practiced.

If regarding the human soul as if it were an angel incarnate is a fundamental mistake (an angelistic fallacy), then that recommendation is also erroneous or mistaken. The body is not the prison house of the soul. Death is not the soul's emancipation, a goal to be sought or approximated before it is attained.

We are left, however, with one further consequence. If it is erroneous to regard the human soul as if it were an incarnate angel, overcoming this angelistic fallacy generates a disturbing perplexity for certain Western religions, especially Christianity and Islam.

Both believe not only in the immortality of the soul, but also in the resurrection of the body. The dogma concerning the soul's immortality is rendered most credible by a conception of the soul that commits the angelistic fallacy. Yet that very conception makes the resurrection of the body obnoxious or repugnant.

Materialism, of course, denies not only the reality and possibility of angels, but also the reality and possibility of an immortal soul. Adopting that philosophical doctrine makes the religious dogma an incredible absurdity.

What philosophical view of the soul in relation to the body or of the spiritual and material aspects of human nature makes it at least possible to believe in the immortality of the human soul and also to make sense of the resurrection of the body as something not utterly repugnant, because it would return the soul to the prison house from which death has emancipated it?

I will try to answer this question in Chapter 12, or at least to indicate the lines along which it may be possible to answer it.

11

If Men Were Angels

(1) Angelistic Politics *

IN THE fifty-first of *The Federalist* papers, attributed to Alexander Hamilton or James Madison, the following passage occurs:

What is government itself but the greatest of all reflections on human nature? If men were angels, no government would be necessary. If angels were to govern men, neither external nor internal controls on government would be necessary. In framing a government which is to be administered by men over men, the great difficulty lies in this: you must first enable the government to control the governed; and in the next place oblige it to control itself.

Wise statesmen that they were, the writers of *The Federalist* papers knew that men were not angels. They knew that for government to be effective, laws must be enforced.

* In this Section on angelistic politics, and in Section 4 to follow on angelistic ethics, a caution must be observed. According to Christian theologians, man before Adam's sin was in a state of preternatural grace. Expelled from the earthly paradise in consequence of Adam's sin, man in the world suffers defects inflicted on human nature by Adam's sin. In neither case does man exist in the purely natural state: before the Fall, he was elevated above the natural plane by grace; after the Fall, he has weaknesses that place him below that plane. Hence, Christian theologians would observe that the comparisons here being made between human beings and angels are not comparisons of the nature of the one with the nature of the other, but rather comparisons of fallen human nature with angelic nature.

Virtuous men may comply with just laws voluntarily simply because the conduct the laws command happens to be conduct to which they are inclined by their own goodwill. But all men are not virtuous. Coercive force must be employed to compel their compliance.

All of this seems so obvious that any contrary view may be looked upon as strange. Yet a contrary view exists. It has been promulgated by eminent writers who have a certain renown as political theorists. It has adherents at the far left of the political spectrum.

Philosophical anarchism is the name for this angelistic fallacy. In the nineteenth century, people called the bomb-throwing assassins of rulers "anarchists." Opponents of existing regimes who resorted to violence were called "anarchists." Today, we call them "terrorists."

That use of the word "anarchist" totally ignores its etymology. Its Greek roots do not connote the use of violence. On the contrary, the meaning they convey is *absence* of government. As the word "monarchy" means rule by one, and "oligarchy" rule by few, so, "anarchy" means no rule at all.

The political theory known as philosophical anarchism is, so far as I can tell, a relatively recent novelty. I can find no traces of it before the nineteenth century, when it makes its first appearance in the writings of William Godwin, the father-in-law of Percy Bysshe Shelley, and somewhat later in the works of two Russian theorists—Prince Alexander Kropotkin and Mikhail Bakunin.

All three advocate the abolition of government itself, not the revolutionary overthrow of this or that established regime. They are a very special breed of revolutionists. The ordinary kind think that man's condition can be improved by overthrowing tyrannical and unjust governments and substituting better institutions in their place. Anarchists think that the improvement of human society can be accomplished only by replacing any and all governments by none at all.

It is not the injustice and corruption of bad government that

they wish to reform. It is rather the evil of government itself
that they wish to remove. That evil lies in the use of coercive
force.

Anarchists believe, in short, that human beings are able to live
together in peace and concord without the application of coercive force. They believe that human societies can exist in which
human beings will deal justly without being compelled to do so
by the police power of the state.

Philosophical anarchists acknowledge that man is a social animal, that human beings are naturally inclined to associate with
one another and that such association confers benefits upon human life that cannot be attained in solitude. It is not society, but
the state and government that they seek to abolish, because, in
their view, the state and government cannot exist without the
exercise of police power and coercive force.

The philosophical anarchists are right about that. No state or
government can exist or long endure without enforcing its laws
and using police power or military force to do so. Their error—
their angelistic fallacy—consists, as *The Federalist* pointed out,
in thinking that human beings, like angels, can enjoy the bless-
ings of society without living in organized political communities
and under governments that not only make laws but also enforce
them.

If all men were friends, Aristotle remarked centuries ago, justice would not be necessary. Out of the love they bear one another, they would be inclined to act for the benefit of one another
and avoid doing injury to anyone.

The society of the good angels in heaven, the theologians tell
us, is one in which the members of the heavenly host live together in perfect concord through the love of one another that is
connatural to them—an endowment of their created natures.
Neither just laws nor their enforcement is needed to preserve
the harmony and peace of the angelic society in Heaven.

If men were angels, the utopia of which the philosophical anarchists dream could exist and prosper on earth. It is a totally
impracticable utopia and a wild dream to be soberly set aside in

the clear light of day precisely because human beings are not angels.

They are not by nature inclined to love one another in perfect friendship. They need just laws to direct them to act for the common good that redounds to the benefit of each, and to prevent them from injuring one another. And, since all are not inclined by acquired virtue to comply with just laws, compliance has to be obtained by resorting to coercive force.

Abhorrence of coercive force did not prevent Bakunin from advocating the use of violence—or what he called direct action—to overthrow existing governments, replacing them by none at all. His bitter opposition to Karl Marx and Marx's followers, especially Lenin, arose from his impatience with the Marxist advocacy of what might be called "Fabian anarchism."

Marx, himself, was bitterly opposed to the Fabian socialists who thought that the ultimate socialist ideal could be achieved by gradual steps and legally instituted reforms. To complete the overthrow of bourgeois capitalism, and to replace it with a dictatorship of the proletariat, Marx advocated revolutionary tactics that included violent measures. However, the dictatorship of the proletariat does not fully realize the communist ideal. It is only a stepping stone in that direction, one remove from the ultimate goal.

That ultimate goal, as Lenin explained in *State and Revolution*, will be realized only when the dictatorship of the proletariat—a benevolent, not tyrannical, despotism that employs coercive force—liquidates itself. When will that occur? When the state can wither away because human nature, which is nothing but a reflection of the institutions under which human beings live, has been transformed by life under communism.

With this institutional transformation of human nature, a "new man" will come into existence. The era or regime of this "new man" will consist of human beings able to live, work, and act together in perfect peace and harmony without the institutions of the state and government, without just laws and their enforcement.

The point to be noted here is that human nature is itself denied. There is no human nature, as distinguished from angelic nature. What is miscalled "human nature" is nothing but the product of human nurture, conditioned by the social, economic, and political institutions under which human beings live.

That being the case, human beings, who are anything but angels under all the historic conditions that have so far existed, can become in the future quite like angels when the transformation of these conditions by communism produce a "new man," a terrestrial angel who, like his heavenly counterpart, lives in love and friendship with his neighbor in a stateless society, without government, law, or coercive force.

The philosophical anarchism of Godwin, Kropotkin, and Bakunin represents an angelistic fallacy in political theory. The Fabian or creeping anarchism of the Marxists compounds that error by combining it with another, equally egregious—the error of denying the determinate attributes of human nature, attributes that determine human institutions and that are not determined by them.

The characteristics that human beings exhibit, under one or another set of social conditions or economic and political institutions, may vary as nurturing develops human nature in one direction or another. What some human beings appear to be like, as a result of nurture, may, at times, conceal what they are really like by nature. They may appear to be, by nature, slaves or inferior, but, as Rousseau pointed out in refuting Aristotle's doctrine that some men are natural slaves, the nurtured appearance belies the natural reality.

Human nature may be affected for better or worse by nurture, but no set of social conditions or economic and political conditions can make men angels.

(2) Angelistic Psychology

As philosophical anarchism is the name for an angelistic error in political theory, so "parapsychology" is the term currently employed for what I regard as angelistic errors concerning the powers some human beings *appear* to possess.

I lay stress on the word "appear," because the reality of the phenomena can be, and has been, challenged. Parapsychology is the study of behavior that is out of the normal—far out! The two forms of such behavior with which I am here concerned are telepathy and telekinesis.

We observed earlier that angelic communication is telepathic in the sense that no physical medium whatsoever is employed in the speech of angels with one another. Angelic thought is conveyed from one angel to another without the use of physical means.

For one human being to plant a thought in the mind of another without using written or voiced words or any other physical means to do so would be telepathic communication. So, too, would be the parapsychological phenomenon of mind-reading, by which one human being can read what is in the mind of another without its being revealed through any physical expression of what is being thought by the other.

It should be added here that theologians maintain that not even the angels, but only God, can read what is in the hearts and minds of men. If the phenomena that claim to be instances of telepathy and mind-reading are genuine (i.e., if observers are not deceived or mistaken in what they report), then we would have to conclude that some human beings—hardly all—have angelic powers of communication, or powers beyond even that.

Why some, and not all? Why does not such power belong to all human beings as a natural endowment? All angels have such power by natural endowment. Why are only some men like angels? No satisfactory answer has ever been offered.

Another explanation of these parapsychological phenomena can, of course, be advanced. It is within the bounds of possibility that the human brain, as an electrical field of force, can send out electrical waves or currents that might explain telepathy and mind-reading.

We have yet to discover the electrical transmitters and receivers and to detect the electrical transmission in the intervening physical medium through which one brain is in touch with that of another. The physical mechanisms may, nevertheless, exist and may be discovered or detected.

If that should turn out to be the case, then mind-reading and thought-transference would not be instances of angelic telepathy but entirely human performances, and performances that should not be the power of only a specially gifted few, but within the reach of all of us.

A purely physical or materialistic explanation of these parapsychological phenomena would not involve any angelistic fallacy. Unaccompanied by such explanation, the acceptance of the phenomena as genuine, not fakes or deceptions, is an angelistic error committed by many people, including some scientists and some philosophers. I am compelled to add that even some of my best friends have shown themselves to be guilty of it.

What has been said about telepathy applies to telekinesis—the power whereby a human being moves a physical body without *appearing* to employ any physical means to do so. This power all angels are said to have. Not all human beings claim to have it. Why it is so special a gift, we do not know.

In any case, if what appears to be going on in observed instances of telekinesis is genuine, we may be able, some day, to give a purely physical explanation of it. No angelistic error would then be committed. Failing to discover the physical mechanisms that authenticate such an explanation, persistence in the strange belief that some individuals have the power of telekinesis makes the believers guilty of this error.

Parapsychology covers one other group of phenomena that justifies calling it an angelistic psychology. Long before the word "parapsychology" came into use, something called psychical research investigated communication between living human beings and departed spirits—usually, but not always, their friends or loved ones.

The phenomena may be spurious, but, if they are regarded as genuine, that involves a belief in the continuing existence of a soul or purely spiritual substance, after death emancipates it from the body.

I have already made clear why I regard such spiritualistic belief as angelistic and fallacious.

(3) *Angelistic Linguistics*

The telepathic communication of which angels are capable naturally enables them to communicate without any chance of misunderstanding. That men and women, not being angels, must use ordinary language in order to communicate makes the likelihood of their misunderstanding one another inevitable and endemic.

The development of symbolic logic or logistics in the last few centuries has resulted in the invention of special systems of notation that differ from ordinary and conventional languages such as English, French, or Russian, in two important respects.

In the first place, these invented systems of notation consist of totally unambiguous symbols. Expert users of them cannot be mistaken about their meaning.

In the second place, their unambiguity is accompanied by the fact that their meaning does not involve reference to anything that exists in the real world or even in the realm constituted by objects of thought or imagination. Expert users of these invented notational systems may be able to communicate with one another without any chance of misunderstanding, but, in doing so, they are saying nothing about any of the objects, real or otherwise, to talk about which human beings use ordinary, conventional languages.

The seventeenth-century German philosopher Gottfried Wilhelm Leibnitz was, in a way, the father of modern logistics and symbolic logic. However, Leibnitz was not satisfied with what might be achieved by the kind of notational systems employed in logistics. He wanted something much better than that. He conceived the possibility of inventing a language he called a Universal Characteristic that would combine one attribute possessed by ordinary language with another possessed by a logistic system of notations.

On the one hand, the invention he had in mind would enable human beings to talk to one another about objects, real or otherwise, concerning which they employ ordinary, conventional languages to discuss.

On the other hand, his proposed invention would enable human beings to engage in conversation about the real world or about objects of thought and imagination without any chance of their misunderstanding one another in the process of doing so.

A nice trick, if it can be done. It is not do-able, of course, because men are not angels. Leibnitz's proposed invention never saw fruition. His belief in what he proposed as a genuine possibility represents an angelistic fallacy in the field of linguistics.

(4) *Angelistic Ethics*

We are instructed by theologians that, in the realm of the good angels, to know and to understand the good is to will it.

Our common experience of human behavior on earth includes the remorse most of us have experienced as a result of having willed the opposite of what we knew to be good. Most of us are aware that we have done things we ought not to have done and have failed to do things we ought to have done.

The best explanation of why this is so consists in recognizing that, in human conduct as contrasted with the action of angels, knowing what is really good for oneself and so knowing what one ought to do does not suffice to produce conduct that aims at what is really good or discharges our obligation to do what we ought.

As human beings, unlike angels, we have both sensitive and intellectual knowledge, and we have sensuous desires and aversions that constitute our bodily passions or emotions, as well as intellectually formed desires that constitute acts of will. Both kinds of desires operate to produce human conduct.

Sometimes our passions overcome our rational judgments, and

then we act to gain sensuous pleasures or avoid sensuous pains, only to acknowledge later with remorse that we did the wrong thing.

At other times, usually less frequent, our rational judgments prevail over our emotional tendencies or the drive of our passions. Then, we will to seek or do that which is really good for us—what we ought to do.

Accordingly, virtuous persons are those who have formed the habit of so controlling their passions by reason that they are generally inclined to will as they ought. Simply knowing what is really good does not suffice for good conduct.

A person can know all the ethical truths that a sound moral philosophy teaches concerning what ought or ought not to be done and still be a thorough rascal or villain. Moral knowledge does not make a morally virtuous human being or lead inevitably to the possession of a good moral character.

To hold, as Socrates maintains in certain of the early Platonic dialogues, that knowledge *is* virtue—that to know the good *is* to will and do the good—commits an angelistic fallacy that is as outrageous to common sense, based on common experience, as are all the other angelistic fallacies that we have examined in this and the preceding chapters.

A moral philosophy that had this as its first principle would be an egregiously erroneous angelistic ethics. Fortunately, no moral philosophy has ever been developed that takes its start from the principle stated above, though I must add that the moral philosophy of Immanuel Kant comes close to being an angelistic ethics. Its rigor and purism are so extreme that only an angel could live according to its precepts.

In one Platonic dialogue, at least, the *Meno*, Socrates takes a position which invalidates the principle that knowledge is virtue—that to know the good is to do the good. Socrates argues most persuasively that moral virtue cannot be taught, precisely because it is *not* knowledge. If it were identical with knowledge, which is eminently teachable, he would have argued in the opposite direction.

However, there is another statement by Socrates that does lead to the development of a moral philosophy tainted with angelistic error. At the end of his trial, after he has been condemned to death, Socrates says to his judges: "Know this, that no harm can come to a good man in this life or the next."

A good man, a man of goodwill, cannot be harmed or injured in any way, because the only thing that is really good, in this world or the next, is a good will. The Stoical ethics of Marcus Aurelius and Epictetus and the moral philosophy of Immanuel Kant affirm that proposition as a first and ruling principle.

What follows from it is that virtuous human beings or persons of goodwill can lead perfectly good human lives and enjoy happiness no matter what injuries and injustices they suffer as the result of misfortunes or at the hands of others or of the society in which they live.

Such misfortunes as physical deformity, ill-health, and under-nourishment can hurt only the body, not the soul or spirit. Such injustices as enslavement, deprivation of schooling, and political disfranchisement do not prevent a man from having a good moral character or a good will.

They are at most accidental evils above which the morally good man can rise. Their opposites are accidental goods, the possession of which is not required for a morally good life. The only essential good, the only thing needed, is a good will.

———————

Some people, including some of the readers of this book, may think it odd for a philosopher (especially one, such as I am, who holds that philosophical thought has its roots in common sense) to be seriously concerned with angels as objects of philosophical thought. They have no place in common experience and are way beyond the reach of common sense.

In response, I would like to point out that a philosophical consideration of angels is not an odd excursion in thought for persons who are addicted to, and respectful of, common sense. On the contrary, both theological speculation about angels as objects of religious belief and the philosophical consideration of angels as possible beings have proved indispensable to exposing the angelistic fallacies at the bottom of a wide variety of theories and opinions.

It is these theories and opinions that are far out, not angelology. Some of them appear to be so strange or weird, at least to persons of common sense, that it is difficult for those of us in that category to believe they have been proposed or embraced by extremely thoughtful men, among whom are some philosophical geniuses—Plato, Descartes, Spinoza, Leibnitz, Berkeley, Kant, Hegel, Schopenhauer, and Nietzsche.

One very important lesson to be learned from the history of human thought is this: no theory or opinion is so strange or weird that it is beyond the power of the human mind to confect and cherish.

PART FIVE

Epilogue

12

Man on the Boundary Line

(1) *Straddling the Line or Reaching Over It?*

THE BOUNDARY line is the line that divides the world of physical, corporeal things from the realm of purely spiritual beings, real or possible.

It was an oft-repeated insight of eighteenth-century English poets, essayists, and philosophers that man occupies a position in between the two worlds. Alexander Pope's *Essay on Man* contains these lines:

> Placed in this isthmus of a middle state,
> A being darkly wise, and rudely great:
> With too much knowledge for the Sceptic side,
> With too much weakness for the Stoic's pride,
> He hangs between; in doubt to act or rest;
> In doubt to deem himself a God or Beast,
> In doubt his Mind or Body to prefer,
> Born but to die, and reas'ning but to err; . . .
> Chaos of Thought and Passion, all confus'd,
> Still by himself abus'd, or disabus'd;
> Created half to rise, and half to fall,
> Great lord of all things, yet a prey to all;
> Sole judge of Truth, in endless Error hurl'd;
> The glory, jest, and riddle of the world!

Another English poet, Edward Young, referred to mankind as a

> Distinguished link in Being's endless chain,
> Midway from nothing to the Deity.

John Locke, and Joseph Addison after him, concurred in placing man at the borderline between corporeal and spiritual beings, but qualified this by saying that the distance from that point upwards to God was greater than the distance downward from it to the least particle of matter.

The placement of man on the line that divides the two realms of being is subject to alternative interpretations.

On the one hand, it can be affirmed as a corollary of the Platonic and Cartesian conception of man as compounded of two distinct and separate substances—one a body, the other a rational soul or intellect. Man, so conceived, stands on the boundary line by being half in one world and half in the other. Being composed of two substances, he enjoys full status in both of these two realms.

This seems to be the view taken also by Immanuel Kant, the eighteenth-century German philosopher. "Human nature," he declared, "occupies as it were the middle rung in the Scale of Being . . . equally removed from both extremes." This conception of man as occupying a "middle rung" or being the "middle link" in the chain cannot be separated, as Professor Lovejoy pointed out, from "the peculiar duality in [man's] constitution." Kant, it would appear, for all his efforts to start philosophy off on a new path, remained a Cartesian dualist.

On the other hand, man's being on the boundary line can be given an Aristotelian, as contrasted with a Platonic and Cartesian, interpretation.

When that is done, man does not straddle the line by standing with one foot in one realm and one foot in the other—equally represented by having his body in one realm and his rational soul or intellect in the other. Quite the contrary! On this interpretation, man stands mainly on the corporeal side of the line and leans over to the other side by the reach of his intellect.

Man, so conceived, is not equally—or half and half—corporeal and spiritual. If one were to count up all his physical and vital powers, the computation would show that he is predominantly a corporeal substance, an organic body, having all the vital powers possessed by plants and animals, but also with an intellect that represents the one immaterial aspect of his being and activity.

That one aspect, very much less than half of the whole, is itself not wholly independent of the much more numerous material aspects. Man's intellect cannot function except in cooperation with and in dependence on his bodily faculties of perception, memory, and imagination. Nor is it free from the influence of his bodily passions.

The action of the human brain and nervous system, as well as the action of other bodily organs, remains a necessary condition for the occurrence of intellectual activity—conceptual thought, rational judgment, and reasoning. What makes the intellect an immaterial aspect of human nature, on the Aristotelian view of man, is the fact that the indispensable corporeal underpinnings necessary for its operation are not sufficient by themselves to explain its action.

The following statement of Thomas Aquinas must be given the Aristotelian interpretation of man's position on the boundary line:

> Man is, as it were, the horizon and boundary line of spiritual and corporeal nature, and intermediate, so to speak, between the two, sharing in both corporeal and spiritual perfection.

We know this, not only from the fact that Aquinas is a self-proclaimed disciple of Aristotle. It is also confirmed by his statement that "the human intellect . . . is the lowest in the order of intellects and the most removed from the perfection of the Divine intellect," in fact, the only intellect that is dependent on a body for its operation.

(2) *The Weakness of the Human Mind*

Unlike minds without bodies, infinite or finite, minds dependent on bodies cannot understand, know, or think without the concurrence of bodily functions.

Furthermore, unlike the intuitive act of the angelic intellect by which the angels also have knowledge of the realities they understand, the intuitive act of the human intellect by which we apprehend intelligible objects or objects of thought does not give us knowledge of reality. We attain that only through the cogitative and ratiocinative processes of judgment and inference.

The angels are purely intellectual beings. We are not. We are rational animals. The angels do not need to think conceptually and discursively. We do. Conceptual and discursive thinking is the lowest form of intellectual life.

In addition, the human, unlike the angelic, mind attains little certitude and what certitudes it does attain are mainly about intelligible objects, not about real existences. Most of the truths we are able to affirm remain forever in the sphere of doubt.

Finally, unlike the angelic intellect, the human mind is the very opposite of infallible. The understanding and knowledge it achieves are always subject to improvement through corrections that can be made by obtaining further evidence and by better reasoning.

All these weaknesses of the human mind would also undoubtedly afflict the extraterrestrial intelligences that certain contemporary cosmologists predict dwell on other planets in this vast universe.

Setting aside diverse estimates of the probability of their actual existence, the possibility of their existence cannot be gainsaid any more than the possibility of angels can be. If they do exist in the physical universe, not in Heaven, then their existence must be corporeal and, therefore, the operation of their minds—with, not without, bodies—would be subject to all the essential weaknesses of the human mind.

Imaginative cosmologists and science-fiction writers are prone to fanciful extravaganzas of a contrary tenor. Allowing their imaginations to run to unreasonable excesses, they sometimes portray extraterrestrial intelligent beings as a step upward from man in the scale of being, as man is a step upward from apes and porpoises, even suggesting that this involves a difference in kind, not just in degree.

That simply cannot be so. The only step upward from man, the only radically different kind of being that is superior to man, is an angel. If there are extraterrestrial corporeal beings that have minds or intellects, they can be superior to human beings only in degree, not in kind. They, too, would be straddlers on the boundary line between the physical world and the realm of purely spiritual beings.

(3) *The Middle Ground*

We are generally inclined to think that the truth about any subject lies at a middle ground between extremes.

One reason for thinking this is that the extremes usually represent conflicting half-truths that can be reconciled and put together to make the whole truth which occupies the middle ground.

The superiority of the middle ground over the extremes between which it lies seems to obtain with regard to diverse conceptions of man or theories about human nature.

In the course of preceding chapters, I have mentioned all of these diverse conceptions or theories or, at least, the principal ones, and have indicated which are the extremes and which lie at the middle between them. Let me now recapitulate what has been said before. I will do so in a somewhat different fashion.

At one extreme, we have two theories, neither of which is dualistic. Neither maintains that man is anything except a corporeal substance, a living organism, differing for the most part in degree from other living organisms. If there appear to be differences in kind between human beings and the higher mammals, such as apes and porpoises, these differences in kind are superficial, not radical. They can be reduced to differences in degree.

Of these two extreme views, both materialistic, one is slightly more moderate than the other. Its moderation consists in its conceding that at least an analytical distinction must be acknowledged between mental and physical processes. Acts of thought are not indistinguishable from acts of the brain; but, though they are distinguishable, they are not existentially distinct. Acts of the brain are not only necessary, but also sufficient for the production of acts of thought.

At the other extreme, we have two theories, one of which is dualistic, the other not.

The one that is not dualistic is more extreme by virtue of its conceiving man as nothing but a spiritual being—the diametrical opposite of the more materialistic extreme that regards man as nothing but a corporeal substance.

The one that is dualistic is less extreme by virtue of its conceiving man as a composite of two separate and distinct substances—a living body and a rational soul or intellect.

It is this view of man that places human beings on the boundary line between the realms of matter and spirit by having them straddle that line with one half of themselves in the realm of bodies, and one half in the realm of spirits.

The more extreme of these two views puts man wholly in the realm of spirit. Both views at the opposite extreme put man wholly in the realm of matter.

The middle ground between these extremes is occupied by a theory of human nature that is dualistic in one respect and not in another. The duality asserted by this theory is not a duality of two separate and distinct substances. It is a bifurcation in the human mind itself—a sharp distinction between the sensitive powers of the human mind (its powers of perception, memory, and imagination) and its intellectual and rational powers (its powers of understanding, judgment, and reasoning).

That bifurcation or distinction does not view man as straddling the boundary line, but rather as reaching over to the spiritual side of the line by the action of his powers of understanding, judgment, and reasoning.

Only by obscuring or repudiating the difference between perceptual and conceptual thought can the more moderate of the two theories at the materialistic extreme regard the distinction between mental and physical processes as merely analytical—distinguishable in aspect, but not existentially distinct.

The Aristotelian conception of human nature—the view that occupies the middle ground between the two extremes on one side and the two extremes on the other—puts man on the boundary line without committing the angelistic fallacies that lie at the heart of theories that conceive man either as a purely spiritual being or as a spiritual substance mysteriously conjoined with a material substance or body.

While avoiding the angelistic errors indigenous at one extreme, it also avoids an equally serious error at the other—the mistake, and all the consequences that follow from the mistake, of obscuring or repudiating a sharp distinction between perceptual and conceptual thought.

(4) *The Resurrection of the Body*

The foregoing critical review of diverse conceptions or theories of human nature shows how angelology—as a purely hypothetical science, based on assumptions in which we may not believe—contributes to our understanding of man.

The Aristotelian conception of human nature, exempt from angelistic errors and their opposites and so able to reconcile the half-truths contained in the opposite extremes, also contributes to the solution of a theological problem encountered in an earlier chapter where the immortality of the soul was discussed.

The mediaeval theologians who adopted a Platonic view of the human soul as a separate spiritual substance, endowed with the power of surviving after separation from the body, had little or no difficulty in defending their religious faith in the immortality of the soul.

However, it is almost impossible to see how they could justify their belief in another article of religious faith—the resurrection of the human body at the end of time and after the Last Judgment.

If death emancipates the soul from its incarceration in the body, if the soul is better off in complete separation from the body, upon the operations of which it does not depend for its spiritual life or action, then there is something abhorrent about a belief in the resurrection of the body, from bondage to which death freed the soul.

The theologians of the thirteenth century who adopted the Aristotelian view of the human soul as nothing but the substantial form of an organic body that actualizes its potentiality for human life faced serious, almost insurmountable, difficulties with regard to the dogma concerning the immortality of the soul.

Not being a spiritual substance in its own right, not having by its nature an existence independent of body, the soul so conceived does not have a natural tendency to persevere in existence after the death that ends human life on earth. On this conception of the soul, the only argument that can be formulated in defense of the religious belief in immortality rests on the slender premise that the human intellect, which is immaterial in its operation, is also immaterial in its mode of being.

In other words, it is that one aspect of man by which he reaches over the boundary line from the material to the spiritual side which provides some support for the claim that when a man dies something of him *can* remain in existence in the realm of spiritual beings.

I have stressed the word "can" because this very weak and slender argument for the immortality of the soul supports it only by showing that, insofar as it is intellectual or rational, it is *at least possible* for the soul to persevere in existence after bodily death.

It does not support the proposition that the soul *actually does* persevere, which is what the dogma declares and the faithful believe. Nor does it, by itself, help us to understand that article of faith.

If the soul in its intellectual and rational aspect were to persevere through God's grace after separation from the body, it could not function intellectually or rationally, since those functions are dependent on the action of bodily organs. Divine intervention would be needed not only to preserve it in existence, but also to prevent that existence from being null and void—an actuality unable to act in any way.

Little wonder, then, that the adoption by Aquinas of the Aristotelian theory of human nature and the Aristotelian conception of the human soul led to his nearly being tried for heresy by the Archbishop of Paris and to the burning of his books at the University of Oxford.

However, the steadfast and heroic adherence by Aquinas to the truth about man as he saw it, which brought him to the edge of heresy, also enabled him to defend the conjunction of two religious beliefs, not one—the two with which the Nicene Creed concludes:

"the resurrection of the body and life in the world to come."

On the Aristotelian conception of the human soul, it needs conjunction with a human body in order to function properly.

According to Aristotle, a substantial form is *in* the matter the potentialities of which it actualizes, just as the shape of the die is *in* the wax on which it is impressed. In the case of the human soul as a substantial form, there is one exception to its total immersion in the matter of the body.

That one exception is its intellectual power. Though this is the soul's slender hold on immortality in separation from the body, it also condemns the soul to be totally inactive when separated from the body.

Here, then, is a reason for the resurrection of the body that saves that dogma from being abhorrent. Divine intervention may be needed to preserve the soul's existence between death and the Last Judgment, and even to prevent that existence from being a life devoid of activity. But that is an unnatural or, perhaps it should be said, a supernatural condition for the soul to be in.

For its immortal life to be thoroughly natural, it needs to be reunited with a body.

What kind of body is envisaged by the dogma concerning resurrection? Hardly the same body with which the soul was united on earth. Because of all the changes it has undergone on earth, that body could not be resurrected; nor could a completely material body dwell in heaven where the communion of saints is believed to keep company with the angelic host.

If not a completely material body, then, of what sort is the resurrected body? The theological answer is: a *glorified* body, the same kind of body that Christ had when, after his death, burial, and ascent to heaven, he returned to earth to be with his disciples for a short span of time. The glorified body of Christ had the immaterial power to pass through closed doors without opening or shattering them.

The dogma of the resurrection of the body thus ceases to be an abhorrent article of faith on two conditions. The first is that the nature of the soul is such that it needs a body to function naturally in the immortal life to come after its terrestrial life has ended.

The second is that life in the world to come—be it heaven or be it hell—is not life in physical space or under physical conditions. Therefore, the body that is resurrected and united with the soul cannot be a physical body, but must be a glorified one.

In dealing with these religious beliefs and the solution of the theological problems they raise, I have gone beyond the province and power of philosophical thought. I have done so because, in a book about angels that treats them not only as objects of philosophical thought, but also as objects of religious belief, it seemed appropriate to do so in order to complete the picture.

13

What More to Read About Angels

ANY BOOK written about a subject that has a vast and highly
diversified literature is incomplete without a bibliography, especially if the author has restrained himself from disfiguring its
pages by dropping numerous footnotes in which books quoted
or authors referred to are cited.

Readers of this book deserve a bibliography not simply because there are no footnotes in it, but for two other reasons. One
is that it will indicate the writings upon which the writer of this
book himself relied—the works by which he was instructed,
challenged, and sometimes puzzled.

The other reason is that, if readers of this book have become
interested in its subject matter, they may wish to go further in
their reading about angels and other related subjects. A bibliography will help them to satisfy such interest.

Extensive bibliographies set forth alphabetically are not readable and are seldom used except by assiduous and conscientious
scholars. I propose, therefore, to provide a discursive bibliography in which I tell readers about some, not all, of the books
that I have read or have resorted to, as well as books of my own,
sufficiently germane to matters treated in this book to deserve
mention.

I will proceed by mentioning books or essays in an order that
follows in a general way the succession of topics treated in the
present book.

(1) *With regard to angels as subjects of poetry, myth, and legend.*

Readers will certainly wish to reread or read, if they have not
already read, three great poems in which angels play central or
important roles: Dante's *Divine Comedy*, Milton's *Paradise Lost*,
and Goethe's *Faust*.

I recommend for their entertainment, as well as for acquaintance with extraordinary flights of imagination concerning angels,
the following works: *The Screwtape Letters* and the trilogy, *Out
of the Silent Planet, Perelandra*, and *That Hideous Strength*, by
C. S. Lewis, published by Macmillan in 1938; *A Dictionary of
Angels* by Gustav Davidson, published by The Free Press in
1967; *Angels* by Peter Lamborn Wilson, published by Pantheon
Books in 1980; *Men and Angels* by Theodora Ward, published
by The Viking Press in 1969; and *Angels in Art* by Clara Erskine
Clement, published by L. C. Page in 1898.

(2) *With regard to angels as objects of religious belief.* First, of
course, readers should explore the relevant scriptural passages in
The Old Testament, The New Testament, The Apocrypha, and
The Koran. Any good concordance to the Bible will help them
to do so. As for The Koran, I recommend the translation of The
Koran by N. J. Dawood, published by Penguin in 1964 (see
especially Chapters 15: 31–48; 17: 61–62; 35: 11; and 86). I also
recommend two secondary sources: *Islam, Creed and Worship* by
Muhammed Abdul Rauf (Washington, D.C., 1974) and *Islam*
by Fazlur Rahman (London, 1966).

In addition, I recommend their using the *Syntopicon* published
in 1952 by Encyclopaedia Britannica, Inc., in association with
Great Books of the Western World. For every topic covered in the
chapter on the idea of ANGEL, Biblical references are cited. I also
recommend their consulting *The Catholic Encyclopedia, The Jewish Encyclopedia*, the Protestant *Interpreter's Dictionary of the Bible*, and *Hastings' Encyclopedia of Religion and Ethics*, in all of
which they will find inventories of scriptual passages in which
angels are mentioned.

Turning from Sacred Scriptures to the writings of the theologians, my suggestions or recommendations are incomplete, but
they may, nevertheless, prove to be of some help.

Among Christian theologians, Augustine, Bonaventure, and Aquinas should be examined for their contributions to angelology as a branch of sacred theology from the Roman Catholic point of view.

In the case of Augustine, I recommend primarily his *City of God* (the citation of relevant sections or passages can be found in the *Syntopicon*). In the case of Bonaventure, I recommend his *Breviloquim*, Part II, Sections 6–8, though I, myself, have relied on Etienne Gilson's excellent exposition of his thought in a book entitled *The Philosophy of St. Bonaventure*, published by Sheed and Ward in 1938.

In the case of Aquinas, on whose theological and philosophical thought concerning angels I have relied most heavily, I recommend reading the *Summa Theologica*. Several English translations are readily available. The passages to be read are mainly in Part I, and in Questions 50 through 64 of the Treatise on Angels and Questions 107 through 114 of the Treatise on the Divine Government. Readers may also find it useful to look up the passages in Aquinas that are cited under various topics in the *Syntopicon* chapter on angels.

I should mention how much I have learned from the Introductions and Appendices attached to the questions in the *Summa Theologica* dealing with angels that appear in the Blackfriars English edition of that work, under the general editorship of Father Thomas Gilby, and published in this country by McGraw Hill in 1970. These introductions and appendices express a twentieth-century Roman Catholic consideration of angels as objects of religious belief, one that differs in important respects from the mediaeval angelology to be found in the *Summa Theologica* of Aquinas.

Among Christian theologians of a Protestant persuasion, the works of the two great writers at the time of the Reformation must be consulted—Luther's *Table Talk*, in *Luther's Works*, Volume 54, edited and translated by Theodore G. Tappert and published by the Fortress Press in 1967, and Calvin's *Institutes of the Christian Religion*, Volume I, Book II, Chapter 14, translated by

John Allen and published by W. B. Eerdmans Publishing Company in 1949.

For an extraordinarily comprehensive survey of Protestant thought about angels since the Reformation, as well as for the extraordinary contribution of his own thought to the whole subject, I enthusiastically recommend Volume III and Part Three of a multivolume work by Karl Barth entitled *Church Dogmatics*, published in Edinburgh by T & T Clark in 1960. The relevant portions run from pages 369 to 531.

Among Jewish theologians, Philo and Maimonides deserve examination. In the case of Philo, I have relied on a book by Professor Wolfson, published by the Harvard University Press in 1947, entitled *Philo, Foundations of Religious Philosophy in Judaism, Christianity, and Islam*. In this work, I suggest pages 366 through 384. In the case of Moses Maimonides, his *Guide for the Perplexed*, of course, and therein Chapters IV–VII, XII–XIII, and XLIX. An English translation, published by George Routledge and Sons, was available in 1928. I believe it has been reprinted many times since then.

I wish I could be more helpful with regard to the great mediaeval theologians of Islam—Avicenna and Averroës. Their works are not readily accessible in English. With regard to their thought about angels, I have relied on secondary sources. The articles on these two theologians in the *Encyclopaedia Britannica* and in *Hastings' Encyclopedia of Religion and Ethics* should be of some help and should provide leads to further study.

(3) *With regard to angels as objects of philosophical thought.* Readers can begin by looking up references cited, topic by topic, in the *Syntopicon* chapter on angels—references citing relevant passages in the writings of Plato, Aristotle, Bacon, Hobbes, Pascal, Descartes, Locke, and Kant. Leibnitz is not cited there because his works are not included in *Great Books of the Western World*, to which the *Syntopicon* was attached. I suggest examining his *Discourse on Metaphysics* (Sections XXIII, XXXIV–XXXVI) and his *New Essays on Human Understanding*, especially Book I.

The mediaeval theologian whose strictly philosophical discussion of angels I have most heavily relied on is, of course, Thomas Aquinas. The modern thinker who, in my judgment, has made the most significant philosophical contribution to the subject is John Locke, in his *Essay Concerning Human Understanding*. Here, I recommend especially a careful reading of Book I; Book II, Chapter I, Chapter X (Sect. 9), Chapter XI (Sect. 11), and Chapter XXIII (Sects. 5, 15, 18–22, 30–37).

(4) *With regard to angelistic fallacies in modern thought, as well as with regard to their ancient antecedents.* The authors I have mentioned as being guilty of angelistic fallacies with respect to human nature are Plato, Descartes, Leibnitz, and Bishop Berkeley. Once again, the *Syntopicon* chapters on MAN, SOUL, MIND, and MATTER will provide references to relevant passages in their works. These *Syntopicon* chapters will also provide references to the opposing views of Hobbes and other materialists. With regard to Cartesian angelism, I recommend Jacques Maritain's essay on Descartes in his *Three Reformers*, published by Charles Scribner's Sons in 1932.

In connection with topics discussed in Part Three of this book, Chapters 9–11, and in Part Four, Chapter 12, I suggest that readers take a look at Aristotle's treatise *On the Soul*, especially Books I and III. For some help in understanding what is written there, I recommend a little book of my own, *Aristotle for Everybody*, published by Macmillan in 1978, especially Chapter 22 and, perhaps, also Chapter 7.

Books of mine, some written many years ago, that have a critical bearing on theories I have either adversely criticized or stoutly defended, should be consulted for much more adequate statements of the arguments involved than I could expound or even summarize in this brief book. I suggest an examination of the following works.

A series of lectures that I gave at the Institute for Psychoanalysis in Chicago in 1936 was published the following year by Longmans, Green and reprinted by Frederick Ungar Publishing Company in 1957. As published, it bore the title *What Man Has*

Made of Man and the subtitle "A Study of the Consequences of Platonism and Positivism in Psychology." Voluminous and lengthy notes that I appended to the lectures as published substantiated the subtitle.

With regard to the opposite errors of Platonism and Cartesianism, on the one hand, and of materialism and positivism, on the other hand, and for a fuller statement of the Aristotelian view that occupies a middle ground between these extremes, I recommend two books of mine. One is *The Difference of Man and the Difference It Makes*, published by Holt, Rinehart and Winston in 1967, especially Chapters 12–15 and the lengthy notes attached thereto. The same book also has an instructive treatment of ways of understanding the distinction between differences in degree and differences in kind. The other book I would like to recommend, though it is more difficult and technical, is *Some Questions About Language*, published by Open Court in 1976. The Epilogue of this book is brief, readable, and germane.

With regard to differences in degree and in kind, and also with regard to essential, as contrasted with accidental, differences, insofar as both topics are related to the philosophical and scientific conceptions of species and specific differences, I wrote a long article that was published in *The Thomist* in April 1941 (pp. 397–449), entitled "Solution of the Problem of Species." I followed this up by an essay published in the *Review of Metaphysics* in September 1952 (pp. 3–30), entitled "The Hierarchy of Essences." In this connection, I also recommend the reading of Professor A. O. Lovejoy's book, *The Great Chain of Being*, the fourteenth printing of which was published by Harvard University Press in 1978. The substance of this book was delivered as the William James lectures at Harvard University in 1933. Here, I suggest especially Chapters III and VI.

With regard to one particular angelistic error, that of philosophical anarchism, I recommend my treatment of that subject in Chapters 6–8 of *The Common Sense of Politics*, published by Holt, Rinehart and Winston in 1971.

(5) *With regard to the difference between philosophical and sacred*

theology as it bears on the difference between a purely philosophical and a theological angelology. In this connection, I have mentioned several times my book, *How to Think About God.* It was published by Macmillan in 1980. Here I recommend only the Prologue and Epilogue.

(6) *Finally, with regard to views of mine concerning the errors and failures of modern philosophy, views that are intimated but not fully explained or defended in this book.* The best explanation and defense of these iconoclastic views will be found in Chapter 14 of my intellectual autobiography, *Philosopher at Large,* published by Macmillan in 1977. Some points made in that chapter are amplified in greater detail in an essay of mine entitled "Little Errors in the Beginning," published in *The Thomist* in June 1974 (pp. 27–48).

Index

Index